CW00869835

Case Studies

Acknowledgements

The author would like to thank a number of people who have helped in the production of this book. Vincent Tidswell made useful suggestions on the first draft, and has been a constant source of encouragement to me. Tim Smith, who drew the diagrams, proved adept at converting my sketchy ideas for diagrams into a professional reality, and his careful attention to detail also proved invaluable. Linda Ellis patiently typed, and retyped, the manuscript. To all of these I extend my grateful thanks.

The author and publishers are grateful to the following for permission to reproduce the material in this book:

Text and illustrations (by figure number)
Applied Geography 3, 1983   (5.9)
Basil Blackwell, 'Atlas of Drought in Great Britain 1975–76' by J. Doornkamp et al, *I.B.G.* 1980   (4.17 a & b)
Faber and Faber *The Weather of Britain* by R. Stirling, 1982   (4.25 a & b)
The Forestry Commission   (5.29)
The Geographical Magazine, 'Geomorphological machine' by D. Brunsden and J. Doornkamp, May 1971   (3.14); 'Variety in deltas' by W. Ritchie and D. Brunsden, April 1973   (3.34)
Longman: *Process and Landform*, by A. Clowes and P. Comfort, Oliver & Boyd, 1982. (Originally after Kiersch)   (3.12); *Human Adjustment to the Flood Hazard*, by K. Smith and G. Tobin, 1979   (3.39) (3.42); *Glacier Hazards*, by L. Tufnell, 1984   (3.79b); *Human Impact on the Ecosystem*, by J. Tivy and G. O'Hare, Oliver & Boyd 1981   (5.3); *Soils, Vegetation and Ecosystems*, by G. O'Hare, Oliver & Boyd 1988   (5.21)
The Ministry of Agriculture, Fisheries and Food, and the Countryside Commission, 'Broads Grazing Marshes Conservation'   (3.43 a & b), (3.45)
Natural Hazards Research and Applications Information Centre, *Natural Hazards Research Paper* 45, 1982   (1.6b)
The Nature Conservancy Council, 'Coast Dune Management' by D. S. Ranwell and R. Boar (Institute of Terrestrial Ecology), 1986   (3.66); 'Is the breeding distribution of dippers influenced by stream acidity?' by S. J. Ormerod, S. J. Tyler, J. Lewis in *Bird Study* 32, 1985   (5.32)
Reuters Ltd   (3.26)
The Sunday Times   (4.29b)
The Times   (4.24)
John Wiley and Sons Ltd, *Coastline Changes: A Global Review*, by ECF Bird, 1985   (3.60)

Photographs (by page number)

Associated Press: 23, 25, 26, 31, 118

Associated Press/Topham Picture Source: 51

Patrick Bailey: 33 (3.1(a), 3.1(c)), 60, 80 (3.88), 156

Cambridge University Collection of Air Photographs: 73

J. Allan Cash: 282 (3.72)

Eric Delderfield: 47

Robert Evans: 138

The Guardian: 78 (3.65)

Hunting Aerofilms: 112 and cover illustration

Hutchison Library: 53; 134

Landform: 22, 33 (3.1(b)), 35, 41, 70, 75, 82 (3.71), 138

Nature Conservancy Council: 80 (3.67)

Ordnance Survey: 48 (3.23), 85 (3.76(a)), 86 (3.77), 87 (3.78)

Sunday Times: 123 © Amrit Roy

Tass News Agency: 163

Vincent Tidswell: 83 (3.73(b), 3.73(c))

The Times: 116

Tony Waltham: 76 (3.62(a), 3.62(b), 3.62(c), 3.62(d)), 85 (3.76(b)), 92

Westermann Verlag: 50

Author's own photographs: 28, 29, 33 (3.1(a)), 38, 84

The publishers have made every effort to trace copyright holders, but if they have inadvertently overlookled any they will be pleased to make the necessary arrangements.

The author would like to acknowledge that the following have been useful as reference and data sources for some of the tables and diagrams:
'Dam Construction – the effects of the Bakalori Dam' by W. M. Adams, *IBG 10*   (Tables 1, 2 and 3 in Chapter 1)
'Trends and Developments in Global Natural Disasters 1947–81', *Natural Hazards Research Paper* 45, 1982   Table 4 and figure 1.6a in Chapter 1)
Geofile 38, (Table 1 in Chapter 2)
'Learning from Mt. St. Helens' by J. Anderson, September–October 1987, *Journal of Geography*   (Table 2 in Chapter 2)
The Thames Barrier by S. Gilbert and R. Horner, Telford Publications, 1984   (3.41)
Process and Landform by A. Clowes and P. Comfort, Oliver and Boyd 1982   (3.48)
The Quaternary in Britain by J. Neale and J. Flesley, Pergammon Press 1981   (3.57)
New Scientist 2.10.86, C. Gemmell   (3.79a)
East Midlands Geographer 6, 1975   P. Morsley (3.37)
IBG 1980, J. Doornkamp et al,   (4.2b), (4.16b, c, d, e)
The Guardian 18.4.88, articles by Martin Walker   (5.36)

Living with the Physical Environment

Sue Richards

UNWIN HYMAN

Published in 1990 by
UNWIN HYMAN LIMITED
15–17 Broadwick Street
London W1V 1FP

Printed in Hong Kong by
Colorcraft Ltd

**British Library Cataloguing in Publication
Data**

Richards, Sue
    Living with the physical environment.
    1. Environment
    I. Title
    333.7

ISBN 0–04–448034–2

Illustrations by Tim Smith
Cover photograph of the coast line at North
Seaton © Hunting Aerofilms

Contents

Preface

Living with the Physical Environment focuses on the physical background to geography and investigates the role of people as agents of change in the physical world. The book makes the assumption that it is vital for pupils to understand the workings of the earth's physical systems in some detail before they are able to comment on, or predict, the effects of human action, or inaction. It is a complementary text to *Understanding Human Geography*, and *Resources and Environment*, both by Michael Raw.

The book has been written taking into account the various reports and documentation leading up to the National Curriculum. Through using this book, pupils will also be building a secure foundation for continuing with geography to Advanced Level, where a lack of understanding of physical systems can hold them back.

Examples are used at a variety of scales, ranging from the local through the British to the international. Varied stimulus materials are provided and pupils are encouraged to use them in different ways. Tasks vary in difficulty, and some are designed to stretch the more able. Pupils should be encouraged to use other sources of information available to them, perhaps from the library, from other geography books and from the newspapers, to provide new examples or evidence.

Our use of the environment is now such a topical issue that it behoves all of us to make sure that environmental education forms part of every pupil's core curriculum. We must however beware of presenting a single point of view, and it has been the aim of this book to set out facts for pupils to evaluate in the light of their understanding of the physical background. I have enjoyed writing the book; I hope pupils and teachers will enjoy working with it.

Sue Richards
Cambridge 1990

CHAPTER ONE

Introduction

Prospects and problems

Think for a minute of all the ways in which your life is affected by the physical environment. The weather might be a good starting point. It affects the food we can grow, the clothes we wear, the energy we use to heat or cool our homes, the holidays we choose, and more. In many ways the environment is a *resource* which we can use in various ways to our advantage. We build holiday resorts at the coast, catch fish from the sea and mine coal from underground. These are just a few of the many resources available to us. The physical environment of the world in which we live offers all sorts of prospects and problems.

Figure 1.1 shows that in addition to being a resource, the environment can also be a *hazard*, causing difficulty or even disaster. Sometimes the way we use the environment can cause a hazard where there was none before. For example, by cutting down trees for fuel, slopes may be left bare, and soil erosion can result, causing flooding along a river (page 52).

Sometimes by using the environment as a resource, we can turn a hazard into a disaster. Farmers beside rivers like the Ganges, for instance, benefit from the fertile soil which is deposited on the river flood plain and which is added to by every new flood. However, by living on and farming the flood plain, they make it more likely that a flood will have disastrous consequences. This idea is illustrated in Figure 1.2. The left side of the diagram shows the river flood as a resource, or benefit, while the right side shows it as a hazard, or cost. This idea is followed up on page 38.

Figure 1.1 Environmental hazards reported by newspapers in recent years.

Many other similar examples, such as the hazards and resources associated with skiing developments in Italy (page 38) are given throughout the book.

Of course, not all disasters are partly the result of human actions. Some are entirely natural, and we can do almost nothing about them. Earthquakes, volcanic eruptions and hurricanes are three examples. Even here, we are beginning to find ways of making these events less disastrous, as you will see later in this book.

Thus the environment offers us various opportunities. As we benefit from these opportunities, we need to realise that there can also be hazards, which may occur naturally, or as a result of the way we use the environment. We weigh up the benefits and the costs, and then make our decision. Before this decision can be made though, we need to know as much as possible about the workings of the part of the environment we are using. We need to know how the parts of the environment are linked together, and how one part affects another, so that we can assess the effects of changes we might make. An example will illustrate this.

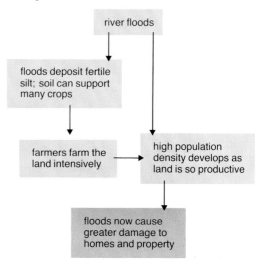

Figure 1.2 Resources and hazards associated with flood plain use.

Systems in the environment

Devonport dockyard, 1987

In 1897, Devonport dockyard at Plymouth was being enlarged and huge quantities of shingle were needed for building works. The shingle was dredged from between the high and low tide levels of Hallsands, a fishing village near Start Point. By 1902 about 650 000 tonnes had been removed. At the same time the beach level fell by about 3m, and boats could no longer be drawn up. Waves started to destroy the sea wall and by 1904 a dozen of the 37 houses had been lost. Dredging was stopped, new sea walls were built and compensation was paid to householders. Then in 1917, disaster struck, as the coast was attacked by 12m waves driven by north easterly gales, at a time of high spring tides. 24 of the remaining 25 houses at Hallsands were removed. Today there are just the shells of a few houses perched above the sea to remind us of the fate of this village. And it seems that the lesson of Hallsands may not even now have been learned.

An eight year battle to prevent shingle dredging off Hastings beach ended in 1988. Dredgers are to be allowed to remove 9 000 000 tonnes of shingle from a bank six miles off shore, instead of the 50 000 000 tonnes they wanted. They are also to be allowed to dredge only where the shingle is more than a metre deep.

Exercise

1 Write down all the ways in which we use the sea as a resource, or as a supplier of resources. Now add a second list of all the hazards you can think of which are connected with the sea.

2 Draw a simple flow diagram showing the knock-on effect of the shingle dredging in Devon, using the words underlined in the text, and the framework in Figure 1.3(b).

Figure 1.3(a) The remains of a house in the village of Hallsands in South Devon.

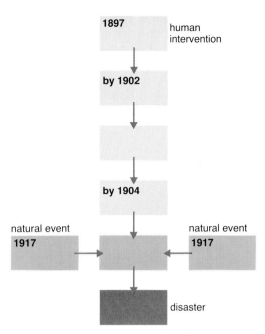

| 1897 | human intervention |

by 1902

by 1904

| natural event 1917 | | natural event 1917 |

disaster

Figure 1.3(b) Framework for a flow diagram showing the processes causing coastal erosion at Hallsands.

The shingle is needed to feed to concrete mixers of the booming building industry in the south east. Protesters argued that the shingle bank might be vital in preventing cliff erosion, by breaking the on shore waves and feeding the coast with protective shingle. Fishermen are also concerned about interference with their nets which are stretched out off shore, anchored to the sea bed. The decision to limit shingle dredging shows some acknowledgement of the workings of the coastal *system*. Today we know more about the energy of the waves, and the importance of the beach in dissipating (using-up) the sea's energy, and we can use this knowledge to control our resource use. (This is covered in Chapter 3.)

So what do we mean by the *coastal system*? A system is a group of items, or processes, which are linked to one another; the human body is a good example. A change to one part of the system will work its way through the whole system eventually. One of the best known geographical systems, which you have probably already heard about, is the water cycle shown in Figure 1.4(a). We can use this example to show that a change which we make can have a knock-on effect through the whole system.

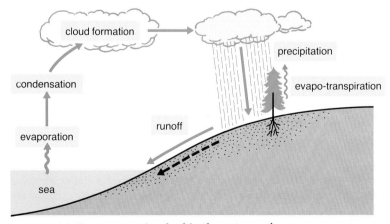

cloud formation

precipitation

condensation

evapo-transpiration

evaporation

runoff

sea

Figure 1.4(a) The processes involved in the water cycle.

Imagine that a huge area is planted with coniferous trees. These trees will transpire more than the grass they replaced, so more water will be lost into the atmosphere. Therefore there will also be less water left in the soil, and less water reaching the river. This sequence of events is shown in Figure 1.4(b).

There are numerous examples of such knock-on effects when one part of the system is changed. In many cases the consequences are human as well as natural; what is interesting is that they often arise from good intentions (see page 162). One typical example comes from north west Nigeria.

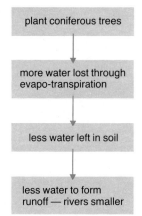

Figure 1.4(b) How a change in the vegetation cover might affect the water cycle.

The Bakolori dam, Nigeria

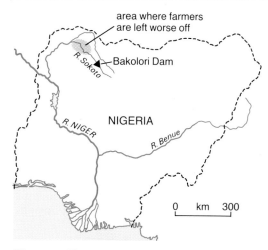

Figure 1.5 The location of the Bakolori irrigation scheme on the Sokoto river in Nigeria.

The Bakolori dam (Figure 1.5) was built across the River Sokoto in 1974–78. The main purposes were to control a strongly seasonal flow and to irrigate 30 000 ha (hectares) of farmland. For the farmers living downstream on the flood plain of the river, the river's discharge fell to about two thirds of its former level. This caused a dramatic change in the type of farming they were able to do.

Before 1978 they grew these crops:

Wet season
a) Millet and sorghum on upland areas ('tudu'), using rainfall.
b) Rice and sorghum on damp flood plain using river water which flooded these 'fadama' plots.

Dry season
Either, a second crop of cotton, ground nuts or peas in the drier areas of the flood plain, or a second crop of vegetables (onions, peppers, potatoes, cassava – all valuable crops) in the wetter areas of the flood plain.

No crop was grown on the upland areas.

The second way in which people used their environment was to fish. Fishing used to take place all year, and fish provided an important source of protein in the diet. Tables 1, 2 and 3 illustrate some of the changes that took place after the dam was built.

So, for example, after the dam had been built only 14% of the plots was used to grow any rice, instead of the 66% previously. In the dry season only 53% of the plots could be used to grow any crop at all, compared with 82% previously.

Table 1   Fadama plots flooded in three villages

	Village 1	Village 2	Village 3
% of plots flooded before dam built	93	79	88
% of plots flooded after dam built	3	28	25

Table 2   Percentage of plots growing different **wet** season crops

Crop	Before	After
Rice	66	14
Millet	35	61
Sorghum	41	75
Maize	7	6
Beans	22	37
Ground nuts	13	19
Cotton	12	16

Table 3   Percentage of plots growing different **dry** season crops

Crop	Before	After
Any crop	82	53
Tomato	38	23
Peppers	40	23
Potato	52	23
Cassava	42	32
Tobacco	15	8
Onion	4	2
Sugarcane	8	4

Exercise

1 Crops like beans, ground nuts and cotton need less water than rice. What happened to the production of these crops after the dam was built?

2 What happened to dry season crop production after dam building?

3 Why was it a particularly important loss that farmers could not grow as many vegetable crops as previously?

4 The purpose of this dam was to encourage irrigated farming. Where are the areas which must have benefitted?

5 The environment on this flood plain has been made *more* hazardous. What disaster could result for these farmers if they are unable to grow sufficient food crops?

The other problem was that after the reservoir filled up, all the villages had reduced catches of fish. Some species of fish disappeared altogether, and in five out of the 23 villages surveyed, fishing had stopped completely.

So do you still think that irrigation is always a good thing? Did you realise that knock-on effects through the farming system could also have such unwelcome effects? Another example, going a stage further, is described on page 162.

Disasters

Disasters have become an important part of geography. This is at least partly because geography, which links the physical and the human systems, gives a good framework for the analysis of causes, effects, and not least, prevention.

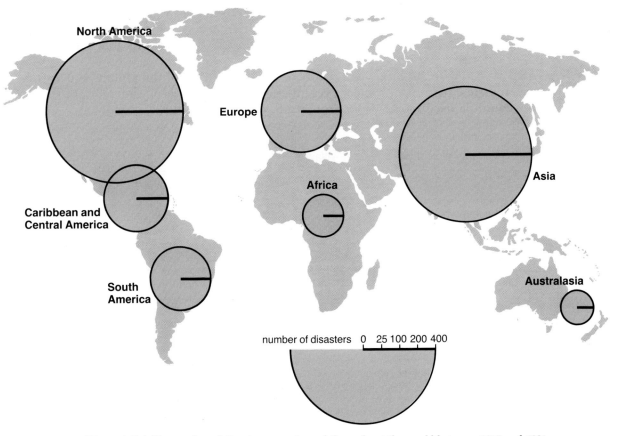

Figure 1.6(a) The number of disasters experienced throughout the world between 1947 and 1981.

Table 4   Disasters by type

Agent	Number of disasters
Floods	343
Hurricanes, typhoons, cyclones, tropical storms	211
Earthquakes	161
Tornadoes	127
Snowstorms	40
Thunderstorms	36
Landslides	29
Rainstorms	29
Heatwaves	22
Volcanoes	18
Cold waves	17
Avalanches	12
Tsunamis	10
Fog	3
Frost	2
Sand and dust storms	2

Exercise

1 Look at the list of disasters which occurred between 1947 and 1981 (Table 4). Divide the disasters into two groups, those which are *climatic* and those which are *geomorphic* (to do with land). Count up the number of disasters in each group and show your results in a bar graph. Did you have any difficulty deciding which group to put each disaster in? Floods may have caused you a problem. You might say they are climatic because they happen after heavy rain, but a particular flood might be worse in a heavily built up area where there are lots of concrete surfaces that don't let the water drain away, and where the drains and sewers can't cope with the extra water. The rock type might be impermeable, making it even less easy for the water to soak away into the ground. So was it also geomorphic? Or did it perhaps have a human cause?

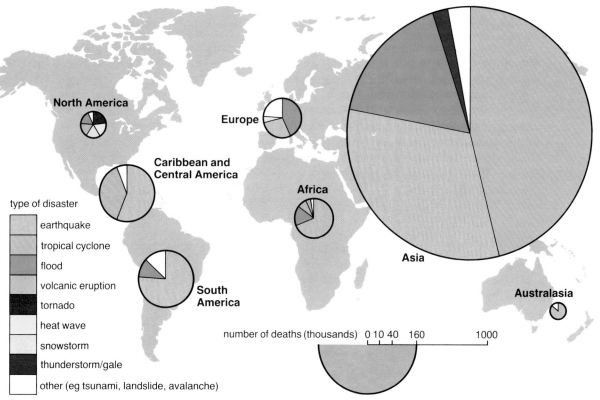

Figure 1.6(b) Loss of life in disasters of different types throughout the world, between 1947 and 1981.

2 In terms of loss of life, which are the greatest disasters?

3 Describe the distribution of disasters in the world, using Figure. 1.6(a). Which areas had the greatest number of disasters between 1947 and 1981? Which areas had the least?

4 What do you notice about the types of disasters causing loss of life in North America? (Figure 1.6(b).)

5 A comparison of Figure 1.6(a) and (b) shows an interesting contrast. Look at North America. What do you notice? What about Asia?

   Why is it that disasters are much worse in Asia in particular, and in less developed countries in general? It is partly to do with the number of people living in those countries. Where there is a high population density, a disaster will have a bigger impact. It is also to do with the degree of risk. The risk of disasters can be reduced in various ways:

a) By preventing certain land uses such as housing or industry in high risk areas, for example on a flood plain.

b) By enforcing certain building regulations to make houses, flats and offices better able to withstand the shock of an earthquake.

c) By predicting when a disaster is likely to occur, so that people can be evacuated, as happened near Mount St. Helens in North America.

d) By ensuring that the risks are appreciated, particularly by people who may not have experienced the disaster in question before. This was a problem with Hurricane David in Dominica (page 118).

e) By looking carefully at the workings of a particular system so that the knock-on effects can be predicted, thus preventing disasters created by humans.

Several of these measures are much easier to carry out in a wealthy country, but much harder to put into practice in a country where there is not enough food for everyone, and certainly no money to spare.

Finally there is one other thing to note about hazards – they seldom have just one simple cause. Several things happening together cause the problem. In the case of Hallsands, for example, it was dredging the shingle as well as the storm which caused the problem. So *people* are part of the environment, we are part of the system, and these systems are themselves linked together. The rest of this book will take you deeper into these environmental systems, and help you to see our role within them.

CHAPTER TWO

The physical framework

The earth was formed about 4600 million years ago. *Homo sapiens* moved into Europe about 50 000 years ago. Think of it like this. If the whole of the earth's history were represented by one 24-hour day, then the human species developed just three minutes before midnight, and *homo sapiens* has only lived in Europe for the last *second* of the day.

Facts like this help us to realise that we are all borrowing the earth and its resources for our short lifetimes. We also come to realise that the earth as we see it today has not always been like this. At first its crust was probably made up of red-hot, liquid basaltic material. There would have been vast amounts of gas, but little of the life-giving oxygen we need. It was not until about 1900 million years ago that oxygen started to be produced in large quantities by the plant life which colonised rock and soil surfaces.

Since then it has changed in several ways which we are only now beginning to understand. The positions of the pieces of land which we call continents have changed. Climates have changed. Rocks are being destroyed and created. These large scale processes provide us with opportunities – resources – and with problems – hazards. They also provide the framework which the rest of the world's activities are based on, so it is important to look at them first.

The rocks of the earth's crust

There are three different groups of rocks which make up the earth's crust. Yet the three groups are all linked. They all have their origin in the red-hot liquid which formed the earth's crust 4600 million years ago. Figure 2.1(a) shows the way in which the rock types are linked.

An example (see Figure 2.1(b)) will illustrate how this rock cycle works. Granite, an igneous rock, is weathered to produce sand (quartz grains) and clay minerals. The sand grains may be carried by rivers to the sea. On the sea bed, layers of sand build up and become compressed, perhaps by mud or silt particles. Over millions of years these deposits harden to form rocks.

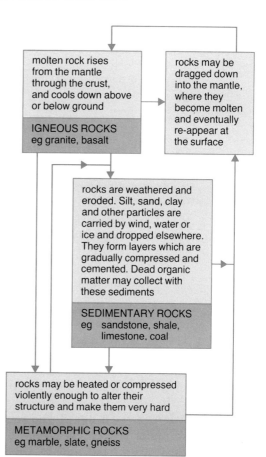

molten rock rises from the mantle through the crust, and cools down above or below ground

IGNEOUS ROCKS
eg granite, basalt

rocks may be dragged down into the mantle, where they become molten and eventually re-appear at the surface

rocks are weathered and eroded. Silt, sand, clay and other particles are carried by wind, water or ice and dropped elsewhere. They form layers which are gradually compressed and cemented. Dead organic matter may collect with these sediments

SEDIMENTARY ROCKS
eg   sandstone, shale, limestone, coal

rocks may be heated or compressed violently enough to alter their structure and make them very hard

METAMORPHIC ROCKS
eg marble, slate, gneiss

Figure 2.1(a) A rock cycle showing how all the types of rock are linked to one another. A single mineral fragment might move through all the stages of this cycle in the whole history of the earth.

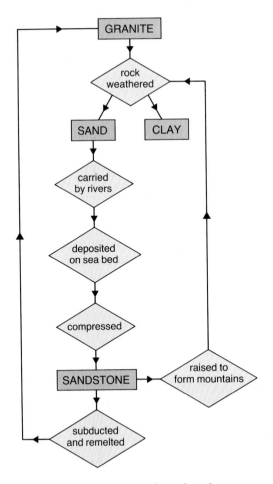

Figure 2.1(b) An example of a rock cycle.

The sand layer may become the sedimentary rock sandstone. Eventually, it might be the fate of these sedimentary rocks to be carried down into the mantle at a subduction zone (see Figure 2.4(b)), where they would melt and recrystallise to form igneous volcanic rock. Alternatively, they might be raised up to form mountains after great earth movements. The sedimentary rocks would themselves be weathered now.

Sometimes sedimentary and igneous rocks are changed by great heat or pressure to form metamorphic rocks. These metamorphic rocks can in turn be weathered to provide the raw material for sedimentary rocks.

One complete cycle would take millions and millions of years. You will notice that there are different routes through the cycle, but that all the types of rocks are linked to one another.

Exercise

1 Look at the following lists of rock types and minerals, and the list of processes beneath them.

Rock types: slate, basalt, shale, clay minerals

Processes: weathering, compression and cementing, severe and violent compression

Link these rock types and processes to produce a diagram similar to Figure 2.1(b). You may add other processes if you wish. Add extra labels and lines to your diagram to show how the rock cycle might continue.

Moving continents: the theory of plate tectonics

The fact that the continents either side of the Atlantic Ocean look as though they should fit together was noticed as long ago as the seventeenth century, but it was not until 1929 that the theory of *continental drift* was put forward by Wegener. At the time it was an unpopular theory, and many scientists argued strongly against it. However, it later became possible to find out the ages of the rocks on the Atlantic ocean floor. The rocks nearest to the middle of the ocean, where there is an underwater ridge, were found to be youngest. Further from the ridge, and closer to the continents, the ocean crust was much older. With facts like these, and with other scientific evidence, most people accept that the continents have moved, and are still moving. Figure 2.2(a) shows how the continents fitted together 200 million years ago, forming a super-continent called Gondwanaland.

Today the theory used to explain the movement of the continents and the structure of the earth is called *plate tectonic theory*.

The earth's crust is divided into 15 plates, of which about seven are particularly large. Each plate is composed of some continental crust and some oceanic crust. Convection currents inside the mantle are thought to be the driving force moving the plates. A comparison of Figures 2.2(b) and 2.3 gives an idea of the importance of the plates in producing some of the earth's features.

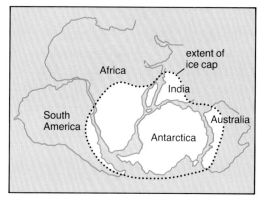

Figure 2.2(a) A reconstruction of the way in which the continents may have fitted together 200 million years ago to form Gondwanaland.

Exercise

1 Carefully trace Figure 2.2(b). Place it over Figures 2.3(a) and (b) in turn. What do you notice? Do volcanoes and earthquakes occur at particular types of plate boundary? Are there any earthquake and volcano regions that are not on plate boundaries? Use an Atlas to name these regions.

2 The present Atlantic Ocean did not come into being until about 180 million years ago. Use an Atlas to work out its approximate width in kilometres today at latitude 40°N. By dividing the distance by the time you can work out the rate of spreading. Is it anything like the rate of 0.5 cm per year measured in Iceland this century?

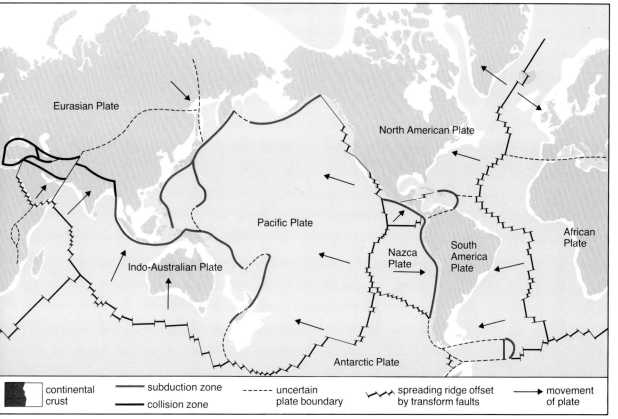

Figure 2.2(b) The major plates of the earth's crust.

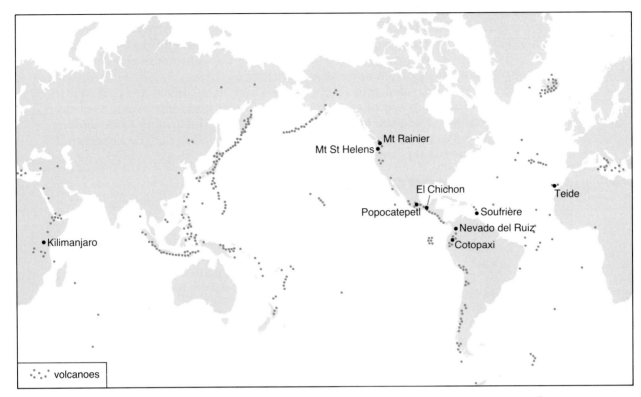

Figure 2.3(a) The world's volcanic zones, with some of the major active volcanoes named.

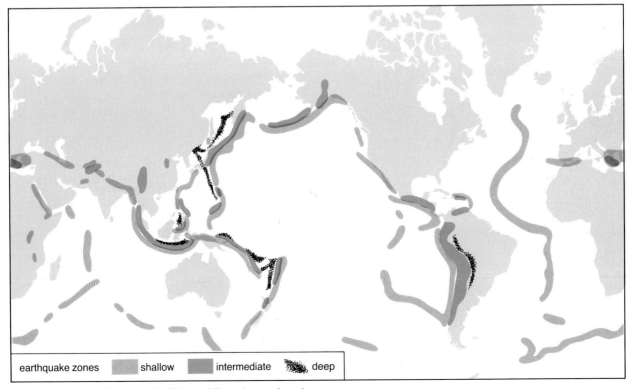

Figure 2.3(b) The world's major earthquake zones.

You will have noticed that most volcanoes and earthquakes are found on plate boundaries. There are two types of boundary where volcanoes are formed:

- spreading ridges – like the mid-Atlantic ridge
- subduction zones – like the west coast of the Pacific ocean.

These two types of plate boundary are illustrated very simply in Figures 2.4(a) and (b). At a *spreading ridge*, currents in the top layers of the mantle are forcing two plates apart. Molten basaltic rock forces its way to the surface where it forms new ocean crust. This explains why the rocks furthest from the ridge were found to be the oldest ones under the Atlantic ocean. Iceland is a visible part of the mid-Atlantic ridge. Its volcanoes are clear evidence of the activity going on below. In 1963 a new volcanic island called Surtsey was born just to the south of Iceland, and in fact Iceland itself is growing as the ridge spreads slowly apart. The rate of growth has been measured as about 0.5 cm per year – barely noticeable you might think. Over 1000 or 10 000 years it becomes more significant!

Because we do not think the earth is expanding, if new crust is being created in some places it must be being destroyed somewhere else. This happens in the *subduction zones*, shown in Figure 2.4(b).

3 Use Figure 2.4(b) to write a description of what happens to the two plates meeting at a subduction zone.

volcano may form over the spreading ridge (eg Surtsey)

molten magma rises to ocean bed and forms new crust

submarine ridge

sea level

crust

heat currents in the mantle

molten basaltic material

mantle

Figure 2.4(a) A type of plate boundary called a spreading ridge, at which two plates are moving apart, allowing new crust to be formed between them.

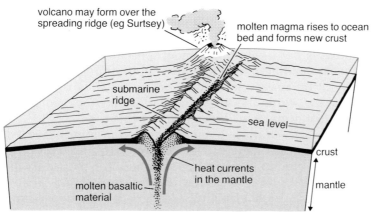

volcanic mountain range (eg Andes)

ocean trench, where one plate is drawn down

sea level

crust

crust

mantle

heat currents carry ocean plate beneath continent plate

earthquake focus, point of great friction between sliding plates

ocean crust melts and bubbles up to the surface, forming volcanoes

Figure 2.4(b) Another important type of plate boundary called a subduction zone. Note that one plate is being dragged down under the other as they meet.

Figure 2.5 Kilauea Iki crater with Kilauea Caldera and Mauna Loa shield volcano behind.

At a subduction zone, both earthquakes and volcanoes may be found. As one plate is dragged downwards there is friction between it and the other plate. The movement downwards is not likely to be smooth, because of this friction. Every sudden move of the descending plate can cause an earthquake. As the plate descends, the temperature rises and the plate melts. Some of the lighter crustal material will rise back towards the surface where it may form volcanoes. The volcanoes of the Andes mountains and Mexico are of this type.

There are two other types of plate boundary shown in Figure 2.2(b). One is a *collision zone*, where two continents transported on plates are colliding. An example of this can be found in the Himalayas, where the plate carrying India is bumping into the Eurasian plate. The other is a *transform fault*. A fault is a fracture in the earth's crust. A transform fault is a vertical line of weakness, or fracture where two plates are moving beside one another at different speeds or in opposite directions. This is what seems to be happening on the west coast of the USA, along the San Andreas fault.

Volcanoes

A volcano is a cone-shaped feature formed where *lava* pours out of a hole in the earth's crust. Lava is the name given to the molten rock *(magma)* as it emerges at the surface. Sometimes the lava will pour out very smoothly, with no violent eruption. In other examples there may be a massive explosion accompanying the eruption.

In general, volcanoes formed in the oceans, at spreading ridges for example, are formed from more basaltic lava. This flows smoothly, and the lava is so fluid that it is sometimes described as a river of fire. Volcanoes like this are often more or less permanently erupting. Excellent examples of this type of volcano are found in Hawaii, seen in Figure 2.5.

Lava which contains more granitic material is much more viscous (ie. it is thick and sticky). It does not flow so smoothly, and often hardens in the central vent of the volcano. This means that next time there is an eruption, the old lava has to be blown out of the way first, and there is an explosion producing rock bombs and ash. This type of volcano seems to be more common at subduction zones where the lava is produced from melted crustal rock. The 1902 eruption of Mt. Pelee was of this type. Figure 2.6 shows another example.

Scientists spend a lot of time investigating volcanoes to improve their understanding of them. From our point of view the most important questions are:

- what hazards do volcanoes threaten us with?
- can we predict when these hazards might threaten us?
- can we prevent a volcanic hazard?
- are there any benefits to be gained from volcanoes?

What hazards do volcanoes threaten us with?

The main threat from a volcanic eruption is loss of life. A survey of disasters between 1947 and 1981 showed that volcanoes were responsible for the loss of 9 457 lives worldwide. This is out of a total of 1 208 002 lives lost in all kinds of disasters in the same period. Since 1981 there have been several more eruptions which have had catastrophic consequences (Table 1).

Figure 2.6 Mt. St. Helens erupting on 18 May, 1980.

Table 1   Recent volcanic eruptions

Country	Date	Effects of eruption
Mt. St. Helens, USA	1980	61 killed by ash fall & mud flow 60 000 tons of ash dumped on western USA Mudflows & floods caused by melting ice
El Chichon, Mexico	1982	100 killed, 500 injured 4000 million tonnes of lava deposited 700 air flights cancelled because of dust
Mount Galunggung, Indonesia	1982	15 killed by lava flows 18 killed by ash emissions 150 000 people threatened by food shortages because of destroyed farmland
Mount Etna, Italy	1983	Lava flows destroyed olive groves, vineyards
Nevado del Ruiz, Colombia	1985	20 000 killed by mudflows & floods caused by eruption of snow-capped volcano

Exercise

1 Find these volcanoes in an Atlas and mark them on a world map. Add the locations of any other volcanoes that you know have erupted recently. At what type of plate boundary is each of these volcanoes found? Are there any volcanoes here which are not located on plate boundaries?

2 Write a paragraph summarising some of the hazards caused by a volcanic eruption.

Can we predict these hazards?

A comparison of two recent volcanic eruptions will help to illustrate the sort of threat an eruption poses, and the chance of predicting an eruption. The two eruptions described here are similar in that they both involved explosive eruptions of ash. Both were snow-capped mountains, and following each eruption the melting snow produced severe mudflows which caused the greatest loss of life.

Nevado del Ruiz, Colombia

On the night of 13 November 1985, this 5400 metre high volcano erupted. (Figure 2.7.) The explosive eruption threw tonnes of ash into the air. The heat from the eruption melted the snow and ice on the mountain top. Flood water carrying mud and ash poured down the mountain side. The Langunilla River beneath the peak became a solid wall of mud which destroyed most of the coffee growing town of Armero, and killed 20 000 of its inhabitants.

Figure 2.7 Colombia, showing the location of the volcano Nevado del Ruiz, and the area affected by its eruption.

A visitor to the area six months later described the scene as a vast desert of solidified mud, a wasteland dotted with hundreds of white crosses with pots of fresh flowers beside them. These mark the sites of houses that vanished with their occupants in the glutinous mud. Cars, buses and tractors lay upturned and half buried in the mud.

One survivor described his experiences when the volcano erupted.

'At six in the evening it was raining volcanic ash and my wife was in a state wanting to leave, but the parish priest said there was no danger, as did the fire brigade. The radio station kept saying that we should all keep calm. I told my wife to stay at home with the kids and I went to my aunt's place on the other side of town to reassure her. At 11 o'clock there was a blackout and I set off home, but I never made it. Waves of mud were sweeping through the town and I only survived by grabbing on to the branches of a tree.'

This man's wife, five children, aunt and 22 other relatives all died. He has never been back to Armero and never will. 'Why didn't they order an evacuation?' he asks.

Well, why didn't they order an evacuation? It is easy to be wise after the event, but there were warnings that something might happen.

For example, in mid-September the Civil Aviation Authority ordered aircraft to stop flying over the mountain because of the quantities of ash it was throwing out.

Figure 2.8 The city of Armero was flattened by the flood and mudslide. Here, a young woman is helped through the mud by rescuers.

On 5 October, the inhabitants of Manizales woke up to find the city covered in a fine layer of volcanic ash.

On 7 October vulcanologists warned that there was a danger of lava flows from Nevado del Ruiz. The government decided there was no immediate danger and took no steps to begin evacuating the town.

Even though scientists thought something might happen, they could not know exactly what or when. Also, the local people weren't very keen on abandoning their homes simply in case something happened, so the government cannot take all the blame.

Mount St. Helens, USA

In this case too there were warnings of the impending eruption. The calendar of events in Table 2 shows the build-up to the eruption on 18 May 1980.

Table 2   Build-up to the Mt. St. Helens eruption

Date	Event	Date	Event
March 22–25	Local earthquakes detected, origin at Mt. St. Helens	April	Area around Mt. St. Helens evacuated. One resident, Harry Truman, refused to leave. Loggers were keen to return to work, because of loss of earnings
March 25	All lands above the timberline closed to public use		
March 27	Small eruption produced crater 10 m × 30 m		
March 30	Glow visible in crater; small ash cloud	April 28	Steam eruptions stopped
March 31–April 12	Steam eruptions; crater, and bulge beneath, grows	May 18	Volcano erupts

Figure 2.9 Damage caused by the eruption of Mt. St. Helens in 1980.

The blast of the eruption felled trees and left them lying like matchsticks on the mountain slopes. Ash was blown 20 000 m into the air. Ice on the mountain top melted and an estimated 46 billion gallons of water flooded down, carrying mud and boulders with it. Some photographers and scientists, together with various holiday makers and forestry workers, were killed, but the death toll was nowhere near as great as that in Colombia.

A sample of people in the Mt. St. Helens area were asked what had been the principal problems caused by the ashfall. A summary of their answers is given in Table 3.

Table 3   Principal problems caused by Mt. St. Helens ashfall

Problem	Percentage of interviewees mentioning problem
Confinement/travel restrictions	59
Clean up	53
Physical health	46
Mental health	16
Economic loss	27
Food shortage	3

Table 4   Some comparisons between Colombia & the USA (1982)

	Colombia	USA
No. of TV receivers/1000	89	646
No. of radio receivers/1000	122	2133
No. of passenger cars/1000	27	551
No. of telephones/1000	65	760
Newspaper circulation/1000	41	274

(Figures per thousand people)

Exercise

1 If a sample of people near Armero in Colombia had been asked about the principal problems that the eruption caused them, what sort of things might they have mentioned? Would the list have been similar to that for Mt. St. Helens?

2 Why do you think there was such a difference in the loss of life in these two eruptions? The facts given about the USA and Colombia in Table 4 might help you with this.

3 What warnings were there that these volcanoes might erupt?

4 What other things should we take into account when deciding if an area is safe from volcanic eruption? For instance, in England we would consider ourselves very safe. Why is that?

Prevention of the volcanic hazard

So far we have looked at the answers to two of our questions about volcanoes. The third question was about the possible prevention of the hazards caused by eruptions. We can't prevent the eruptions, but perhaps we can limit their disastrous effects.

In a postscript to the Mt. St. Helens eruption, one writer noted that 'we build many of our own disasters by taking over and using land which we should respect as areas of natural processes. The splendour and fury of high energy areas makes them both very hazardous for permanent development, and extremely interesting to visit. Mt. St Helens should be excluded from permanent development and preserved for recreational appreciation.'

When people insist on living on the slopes of a volcano, as they do in Sicily for example, they must accept that sometimes the lava will cause loss of land and perhaps of life. The attraction of the slopes of Mt. Etna to farmers is the fertile soil which has developed on the old lava flows. Attempts have been made in Sicily to divert the flow of lava, using bulldozers to open up a new channel for the lava and divert it from its existing course. However, attempts like this are not only very dangerous, but also not usually very successful.

5 a)   What do you think a government should do to prevent loss of life in an area where there are volcanoes which might be active? Make a list of things that should be done.
b)   What types of land use or development should not be allowed in such an area? How would the rules be enforced?

6 Question 5 is about long term planning. What short term emergency plans are needed in an area with active volcanoes? Think about how the Colombian peasants could have been spared the worst effects of the eruption of Nevado del Ruiz. Write a list of points which should be covered in a government's emergency plans.

Volcanoes as a resource

Clearly volcanic areas are very hazardous, but they are also sometimes seen as a resource. One advantage of them has already been mentioned – the very fertile soil which develops on volcanic ash and lava. Java, an island in Indonesia, has one of the highest rural population densities in the world, partly as a result of its fertile volcanic soils.

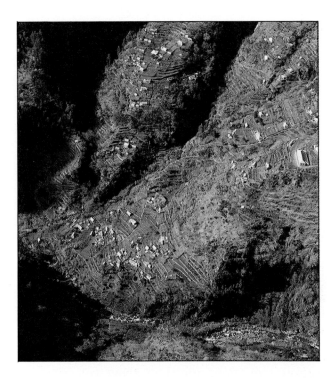

Figure 2.10 Terracing makes the most of the steep but fertile volcanic slopes in Madeira.

Secondly, volcanic areas may be a rich source of minerals. If a particularly metal-rich piece of oceanic crust is melted deep inside the earth, solutions containing this mineral can bubble towards the surface and gradually produce concentrations of that mineral. If enough of the mineral is deposited it will form a workable ore. There are numerous examples of these mineral deposits close to the Pacific ring of fire.

- Cripple Creek, Colorado, USA, was the scene of a gold rush in 1900.
- Comstock Lode, Nevada, USA, experienced a mining boom in the 1870s when silver was discovered.
- Cerro Rico (Hill of Silver), Bolivia, was discovered in 1544. The silver deposits have been mined, but tin is now being mined instead.
- El Teniente, Chile, is one of the largest underground mines in the world, producing copper.
- Aucanquilcha, Chile, is a sulphur mine, the highest mine in the world.
- Bougainville, Papua New Guinea, is one of the largest open cast copper mines in the world.

Thirdly, volcanic areas are now being investigated for signs of hot water underground which can be used to generate electricity. There are already geothermal power stations in Italy, New Zealand and the USA. In fact, Italy's geothermal power station at Lardarello supplies about 3% of the country's total electricity requirements. There are about 100 boreholes there, delivering steam at roughly 230°C. In Iceland, homes and greenhouses are heated by hot water taken from under the ground.

Figure 2.11(a) Minerva Terrace, Yellowstone National Park, USA. This terrace is formed by springs which deposit minerals as the warm water emerges from underground.

Volcanoes, and areas of volcanic activity attract tourists, and this is a fourth way in which they can be seen as a resource. Italy's volcanoes provide good examples. It is possible to catch a bus to the slopes of Vesuvius near Naples, and from the car park a chair-lift carries visitors to the edge of the crater. From here they can walk around the rim of the crater and peer into it. Intrepid tourists descend a few feet to experience warm air and steam emerging from holes called fumaroles in the side of the crater. Mt. Etna in Sicily also attracts numerous tourists every year, but it is a more active volcano and some visitors have lost their lives in recent years from lava unexpectedly pouring out.

Yellowstone Park in the United States is another area which owes much of its attraction to its volcanic features. The geyser, Old Faithful, is famous, but there are also mud volcanoes and wonderful terraces created by mineral-rich hot springs.

Figure 2.11(b) Grand Geyser erupting in Yellowstone National Park, USA.

Exercise

1 Design a poster or wall display, either alone or in groups, with the title 'Volcanoes – friend or foe?' Collect pictures from magazines or travel agents to illustrate your work. Use maps and diagrams drawn from this or other sources. Try to show both the resources offered by volcanoes (the benefits) and the hazards posed by them (the costs).

2 There are conflicts of interest in developing an active volcanic area for tourism. For example, a government official might have a view very different from a property developer or hotel manager.
   a) As a government official what regulations would you enforce to ensure the safety of tourists?
   b) Do you think that the development of tourism should be allowed in volcanic areas?

Earthquakes

An earthquake is a signal to us that the crust is moving. If you live near a busy main road you may feel your house shake as a heavy lorry goes past. That small amount of movement could be detected by a seismograph. A seismograph is a very sensitive instrument used for detecting movements in the earth's crust. In hundreds of stations all over the world seismographs constantly record, on a graph, the movements of the crust. When an earthquake happens, it is recorded at different times all over the world. This is because it takes time for shock waves to travel around the world through the rocks. The strength (magnitude) of each earthquake is measured by the size of the shock waves recorded on the graph. Magnitude is measured on the Richter scale.

The map on page 20 shows the areas of the world where earthquakes are most frequently found. Table 5 records all the earthquakes and tremors which were mentioned in *The Times* in 1986.

Table 5   All earthquakes and earth tremors mentioned in *The Times* in 1986

Date	Location	Effects
28.1.86	N. California, USA	
31.3.86	Aegean Sea, Greece	
1.4.86	San Francisco, USA	
7.4.86	Cuzco, Peru	11 villages damaged
1.5.86	Mexico City, Mexico	
5.5.86	Khanji area, Iran	
6.5.86	S. Turkey	Eight killed, 40 injured. Surgu reservoir drained as a precaution
9.5.86	Aleutian Is., USA	
9.7.86	Palm Springs, USA	
1.9.86	Moldavia, Romania	
14.9.86	Kalamata S. Greece	19 killed, 300 injured. 70% of buildings damaged
17.9.86	Tadjikstan, USSR	
11.10.86	San Salvador, El Salvador	1000 killed, many in shanty town
13.10.86	Shiraz area, Iran	
13.10.86	Izu peninsula, Japan	
13.10.86	Lima, Peru	
14.10.86	Sicily, Italy	
21.10.86	Seafloor near Kermadec Is.	New Zealand on alert because of tidal wave threat
15.11.86	Taiwan	16 killed, many injured by landslides
22.11.86	Tokyo and E. Japan	Earthquake linked to eruption of Mt. Mihara
22.11.86	N. California, USA	
9.12.86	Bulgaria	Two killed, 60 injured

Exercise

1 On a world map mark all the sites mentioned in Table 5 with a coloured symbol. Add to your map any more recent earthquakes which you know of. Does the pattern resemble that in the map on page 20?

2 Do you notice anything about the dates on which earthquakes were recorded?

3 Build up a file on earthquakes yourself, by collecting information from newspapers and magazines.

The Mexican earthquake, 1985

At about 7.20 a.m. on 19 September 1985, Mexico was struck by an earthquake with a magnitude of 7.8 on the Richter scale (see Figure 2.12). Buildings swayed, then collapsed; cracks appeared in the street; waves 20 m high surged up in the sea above the centre of the earthquake and ships were lost; explosions and fires occurred as petrol stations blew up and gas mains were fractured; landslides occurred on mountain sides, engulfing villages. Official estimates say that 6000 people died, others say the total may have been as high as 20 000. 130 000 people were made homeless and two months after the event 20 000 people were still living in tents. After the earthquake was over, the main threat to people was through water-borne diseases such as typhoid and cholera, as the city's water supply and sewage disposal system had been disrupted.

Only two weeks before the disaster, an article appeared in a magazine warning that an earthquake could happen in this area. Scientists had noticed that a band along the south west coast of Mexico had suffered earth tremors, except for one gap a hundred miles wide. They thought that tension might be building up in this one gap, and they were right. The earthquake happened exactly in the middle of the gap.

Figure 2.12 The Hotel Regius lies crumbled in a Mexico City Street.

Tsunamis

An earthquake beneath the sea can cause an additional hazard – a tsunami. This is a huge wave, or series of waves, which forms out at sea and builds up as it moves towards the coast. Most tsunamis are no more than 10 m high, although even this is disastrous enough. Two of the greatest tsunami disasters were in Japan in 1896 and 1933. In 1933, 30 000 people were killed by waves 20 m high.

A more recent tsunami struck Japan in May 1983. Its cause was an earthquake with a magnitude of 7.7 on the Richter scale, in the Sea of Japan. The worst effects of the tsunami were felt at Noshiro harbour on the west coast of Hokkaido. Here there were waves 6–8 m high, with enormous strength. Concrete blocks which had been put down along the coast to dissipate (absorb) the energy of the waves were carried as far as 150 m inland. Each block weighed four tonnes! A hundred people were killed by this tsunami, mainly harbour construction workers, but also fishermen, tourists and even five paddy farmers working in their fields.

Prediction and prevention

We know that the earth's crust is always on the move. We cannot stop it moving, but we might be able to prevent some of the disastrous effects of earthquakes. Read through the following points about earthquakes, then use them to answer the questions which follow.

- Animals and birds have been known to change their behaviour before an earthquake. Snakes, worms and pheasants all seem to be sensitive to slight changes before an earthquake happens.
- Gaps in which no earthquakes have happened can be spotted by scientists, as happened at Mexico.
- Water levels in wells often change just before an earthquake.
- Steel structures which have some flexibility built into them survive an earthquake better than poorly-bonded concrete buildings.
- Shanty houses built of any material locally available offer little resistance to shaking or landslides.
- Fault lines along which movement could take place can be mapped.
- Areas of unconsolidated sands and silts shake too easily in an earthquake; solid bedrock is more stable.

Exercise

1 Which of these things would help us to predict *when* an earthquake might happen?

2 Which would help us to predict *where* it might happen?

3 If an earthquake can be predicted, how could loss of life be reduced?

4 What does the list suggest we could do about building and land use regulations to prevent earthquake damage?

5 What evidence is there that people in poor countries are more likely to suffer from the effects of an earthquake than people in rich countries? Table 5 on page 30 should provide you with some examples to support your answer.

CHAPTER THREE

Landscapes

You probably cannot see much of the physical landscape from your classroom, so instead, look at the four photographs in Figure. 3.1. Each shows a landscape found in Britain.

Figure 3.1(a) The Cuillins from Beinn Cleat, Skye.

Figure 3.1(b) The Seven Sisters, vertical chalk cliffs on the south coast of England.

Figure 3.1(c) Dorset chalk downland.

Figure 3.1(d) A river cliff undercut by Dalby Beck in the North York Moors.

Exercise

1 Choose one of the photographs from Figure 3.1 and write between four and six lines describing the landscape, giving as much detail as you can. Refer to the height and slope of the land, the vegetation cover, and the appearance of the rock. Read out your description to others in your group.

Could they tell which photograph you were describing?

When several people have read their descriptions, make a list of the sorts of things mentioned; for example most people probably said something about slopes, or about the height of the land.

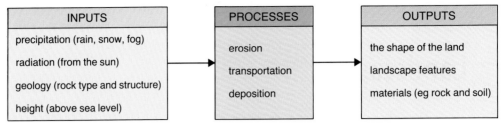

Figure 3.2 Some of the elements which are common to different landscape systems.

Although they look different, the landscapes on the previous page do all have things in common. They can all be seen as a 'system', with the shape or appearance of the land as one of the outputs of that system. (Figure 3.2.) What about the inputs? You can probably think of several. For example, rainfall (or snowfall) is an input to all of these landscape systems. The geology (the rock type and its structure) is also an input. Radiation from the sun will be a third. Note that the four systems will not have exactly the same inputs, but the basic framework is similar.

Within each system are processes which convert the inputs to outputs. Again, some of the processes are ones common to each system. For example, soil or other material may be transported through the system. This could happen because water carries it, or simply because the force of gravity makes it fall.

Material may be taken right out of one system, and then used as input to another. The soil carried down the slope system may eventually get into a river, and form an input to that system. Note that the landscape itself is one of the outputs of these systems.

Remember that systems can operate on many different scales, from a river cross-section up to a whole drainage basin like that of the Amazon. All of these systems are linked together, and form part of the whole 'planet-earth' system.

So far, one other input, and a potentially very important one, has been omitted. If the photographs in Figure 3.1 had shown, for instance, a breakwater, a dam, or terraced hillslopes, you would probably have immediately mentioned this additional input – PEOPLE! There are very few landscapes today which don't show some evidence of the effect of people, even when it isn't obvious. Figure 3.1(c) shows a farmed landscape. By the way that they plough the land, and even when it is sown, farmers can have a huge effect on the shape of the landscape. This effect can be deliberate, such as when a dam is built across a river, or it can be accidental, like a motorway cutting that is made too steep, so a landslide occurs on it. This idea of the environment being both a resource and a potential hazard will be followed up in the rest of this chapter, which deals with some important landscape systems separately.

The Slope System

The landscape we see is made up of slopes. A slope can be anything from a vertical bare rock-face to a nearly level alluvial flood plain covered by a metre of soil. In between many different forms and shapes are possible.

Exercise

1 Look back at the slopes in Figure 3.1. Sketch each one, and label your sketches to show whether the slope angle is steep or gentle, the type and amount of vegetation cover, amount of soil cover, and presence of bare rock.

2 Which photograph shows slopes on a very hard, resistant, rock? Explain your answer.

Artificially created slopes

Mining industries often produce waste which must be dumped, and these spoil tips are a form of artificial slope. The almost lunar landscape in Figure 3.3, of land near St. Austell in Cornwall, is the result of spoil tips connected with the china clay mining industry. Coal mining also produces spoil tips, but some of these have

Figure 3.3 These china clay spoil-tips near St. Austell in Cornwall are slopes created by people.

Figure 3.4 Restoration of a tip at Sutton Colliery in Nottinghamshire. Grass has been planted to the right, and barley is being harvested in the centre. The area on the left is about to be covered with soil ready for planting.

been so well disguised now that their origin would hardly be recognised. Hanley Central Forest Park in the Potteries, Staffordshire, is a former colliery site which is now a popular local attraction.

Many coal tips have been flattened and spread out, so that they are not very high. Then they can be grassed or forested and used for recreation, for example in the Dare Valley country park, where two collieries used to exist.

In other examples, tips are being used for agriculture. Figure 3.4 shows restoration at Sutton Colliery, north Nottinghamshire. Grass is growing on the right, and barley is being harvested in the centre. To the left, mounds of top soil are ready to spread across the shale on the left.

Rock weathering

When rock has been broken up, it can be moved down-slope by water, wind or gravity. If the weathered material moves mainly because of the force of gravity, we call this *mass movement*. If the wind or water carries weathered material away, we call it *erosion*.

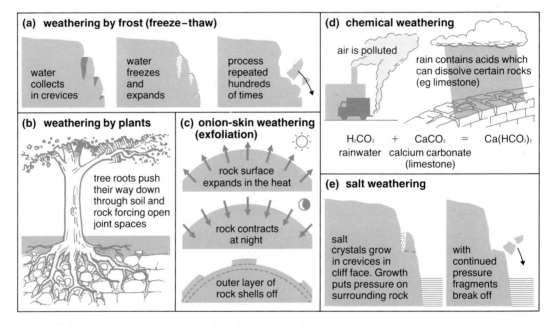

Figure 3.5 Some of the processes involved in the breaking down, or *weathering,* of rocks.

3 Look carefully at Figure 3.5 which shows the way in which rocks are *weathered*, or broken up. Which types of weathering are probably happening on the slopes in Figure 3.1? What evidence did you use to decide?

4 Weathering is an important process in the slope system. It breaks up the rock so that it can be moved by water, wind or gravity. Look carefully at Figure 3.5 and name four factors which affect the type of weathering that will happen at a particular place.

Mass movement

Mass movement ranges from a sudden, rapid event like a landslide, to the very slow, almost unnoticeable creep of soil down a hillside. It can happen with no water present at all, as when there is a rockfall, or there may be a lot of water saturating the soil so that it flows down hill. Figure 3.6 illustrates these four types of mass movement.

Figure 3.6 Four different types of mass movements, by which soil and rock move downhill.

(a) Rockfall

steep cliff

scree made up of rock fragments

(b) Landslide

scar

slumped block of land

(c) Solifluction

lobe of mud and soil which flows down the slope

(d) Soil creep

soil particle expands away from the surface when wet. As it contracts it moves vertically downwards

terracettes on hillside

wall built across slope

In fact water has a role to play in many sorts of mass movement. Figure 3.7 shows a slope which could suffer a landslide, but at the moment the strength of the material is enough to stop the slide happening. If something happens to increase the stress, and the stress becomes greater than the strength of the rock, a slide results. Figure 3.9 illustrates several ways in which this could happen.

Exercise

1 What sort of weathering processes might prepare the rock to fall and produce scree?

2 What would probably happen to the scree if the slope in Figure 3.6(a) were at the coast, being attacked by waves?

3 What is the main difference in appearance between a *slide* and a *flow*?

4 Use Figure 3.6(d) to explain what causes *soil creep*.

5 What evidence might there be to show that soil creep is happening on a particular slope?

6 In which of these sorts of mass movement is the presence of water important?

Figure 3.7 Stress and strength in a slope.

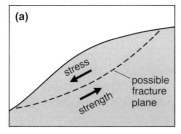
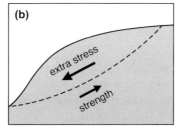
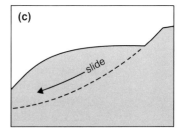

strength = the ability of the material to hold its position
stress = the force encouraging material to slip downwards

Figure 3.8 A landslip west of Edale in Derbyshire.

Figure 3.9 Three possible causes of a landslide.

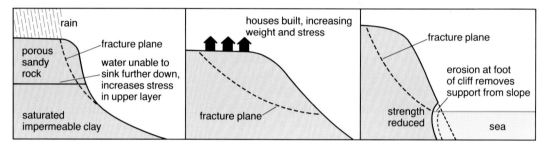

7 Read the following descriptions of landslides which have occurred, and decide which of the three possible causes shown in Figure 3.9 was responsible. In some cases you may decide two or even three were responsible.

A Landslides have occurred several times at Barton-on-Sea where sea cliffs are cut in soft clays. A slide on 17 April 1975 left homes perched perilously on the cliff edge.

B A landslide in 1982 at Ancona, Italy, damaged 785 homes, and various shops, factories and other services. The town is built on relatively soft clay, and is on the Adriatic coast, where beach material is constantly being removed by longshore drift, resulting in cliff erosion.

C In September 1976 the Bristol – South Wales railway line was closed at Patchway by two landslides in a deep railway cutting. These landslides followed a period of very heavy rainfall marking the end of the extreme drought that summer.

D Rio de Janeiro in Brazil suffered severe landsliding on 20–21 February 1988, when one tenth of the city's annual rainfall fell in one day. Many 'favelas' (shanty houses) built on steep slopes surrounding the city were carried away by the slides. At least 200 people died in the disaster.

8 Were any of these landslides the direct result of human activities? If so, say which and suggest how each could have been prevented.

Slope hazards

Valtellina Valley, Italy

As slopes are increasingly used by people for more activities, so the risk of disasters on the slopes increases. In July 1987 the Valtellina Valley in Northern Italy was affected by avalanches of mud, severe flooding and landslides. The map in Figure 3.10 shows the affected area. The factors contributing to this disaster are listed in Table 1. They can be fitted into the flow diagram outline provided by Figure 3.11.

Table 1   Labels for flow diagram.

- Steep mountain slopes already unstable and liable to landslips.
- Ski resorts developed on snow-covered mountain slopes.
- Trees are cut down to provide timber for buildings and to make way for ski runs, cable cars, roads, holiday buildings.
- Runoff from the concrete surfaces of the resorts and roads is more rapid; water gets into streams more quickly.
- Freak torrential rain in July 1987.
- Most of the slopes are naturally forested; helps to protect against landslides.
- Slopes around the resorts are unprotected; snow can collect to greater depths; no root mat to hold soil in place.

Figure 3.10 The Valtellina valley in the North Italian Alps, showing the area affected by avalanches and mudslides in July 1987.

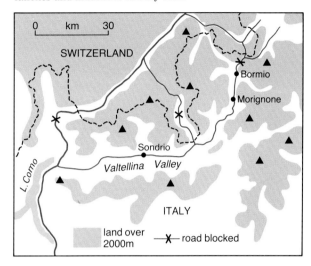

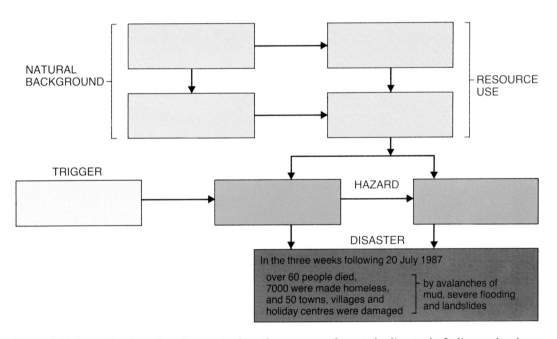

Figure 3.11 An outline for a flow diagram to show the sequence of events leading to the Italian avalanche disaster.

Exercise

1 Make a larger copy of the flow diagram outline from Figure 3.11 and fill in the boxes using the factors in Table 1. To help you to do this, note that there are:
   - two labels relating to the natural background;
   - two labels concerning resource use;
   - one event that triggers the disaster;
   - two hazards that are caused by the resource use plus the trigger.

2 Suggest how the Valtellina Valley disaster might have been prevented.

The example shows that slopes form part of other landscape systems, and in the next three sections they will be mentioned several times.

The Vaiont Dam disaster, Italy

Another example of the link between the slope system and the river system is given by a study of the Vaiont Dam disaster. Figure 3.12(a) shows a geological cross-section of the area in Northern Italy where a dam had been built across the Vaiont River. The dam site was chosen because here the river was narrow and gorge-like. Unfortunately some of the surrounding rocks were very porous. After heavy rain one night in October 1963, a huge mass began to slide downhill

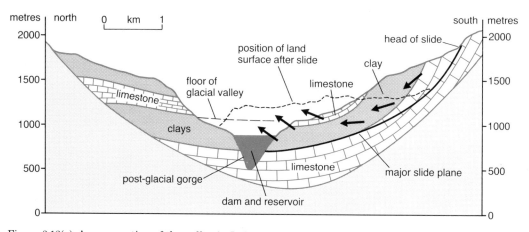

Figure 3.12(a) A cross section of the valley in Italy across which the Vaiont Dam was built.

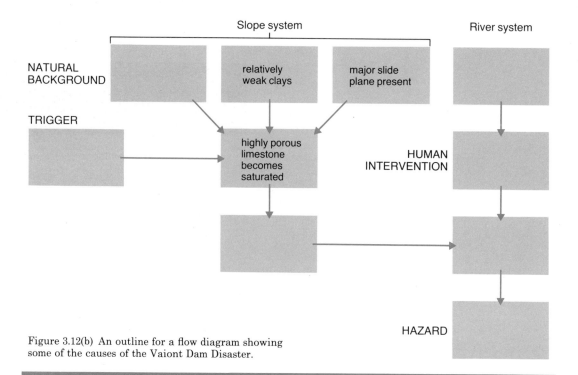

Figure 3.12(b) An outline for a flow diagram showing some of the causes of the Vaiont Dam Disaster.

towards the reservoir. It swept into the river, creating huge waves so that <u>water was forced over the top of the dam and down the valley</u>. <u>2000 people were killed by the floodwater</u> and it engulfed the village of Langarone.

3 Study Figure 3.12(a), then draw a flow diagram, using Figure 3.12(b) as an outline, to show the sequence of events in this disaster. Use the labels underlined in the description above. The terms you need are not printed in exactly the right order to fit the boxes. Shade in one colour the boxes applying to the river system, and in another colour the slope system boxes. What links the two systems?

Soil erosion

This is a process which happens when water carries weathered material down the slope, or when the wind carries soil away. The amount of soil erosion is linked very strongly to the amount of vegetation on the slope, so this topic will be dealt with fully on page 131. Figure 3.13 shows the effect of extreme soil erosion on slopes in Britain – we are used to seeing gullies like these in the badlands of the USA, or the borders of the desert in Ethiopia, but we don't always associate them with Britain.

Figure 3.13 Gully erosion following heavy rain on boulder clay soil near Bungay, Suffolk.

These examples show clearly that landscape systems are closely inter-linked, and that the effects of one event can be very far reaching. It also leads us into the second of our landscape systems – the river basin.

The river system

Rivers have shaped much of the landscape in Britain. Figure 3.14 illustrates their part in the 'erosion machine.' They saw, file, and grind away at the surface of the earth, gradually wearing it away and carrying the debris down to the sea. The energy to do this comes originally from the sun: the sun heats the sea and evaporates water from it, and the water later falls as rain on the land.

Figure 3.14 The Geomorphological Machine. The heat from the sun drives the machine. Water is evaporated from the sea, and later falls as rain on the land. Rivers erode the land surface, while the sea grinds away at the coast. (after Brunsden and Doornkamp)

How do rivers begin?

River water originally comes from the sea or lakes via evaporation, and eventually ends up back there. However, any particular raindrop could follow one of numerous different paths through the *drainage basin*.

Exercise

1 Copy the flow diagram (Figure 3.15(b)) of the drainage basin water cycle, and use Figure 3.15(a) to fill in the boxes. Then answer these questions.
   a) Where precisely can water be stored in the drainage basin?
   b) In what two ways can water leave the drainage basin?
   c) Describe one very short path for a water droplet through the drainage basin, and one very long path.
   d) By how many different routes can water get into the river?

2 Looking at Figure 3.15(a), write down whether these statements are true or false.
   (i)   The amount of water that could be stored in a drainage basin would increase if more trees were planted.
   (ii) If the soil were eroded away, less water would be stored in the drainage basin.
   (iii) A concrete car park built in the drainage basin would mean more water could be stored in the drainage basin.
   (iv) Impermeable rock will increase the amount of water that can be stored in the drainage basin. (Impermeable rock won't allow water to pass through it).

Figure 3.15 Two ways of looking at the drainage basin water cycle.

(a) Here the stores for water are shown in a typical river basin, and the inputs and outputs are clearly shown.

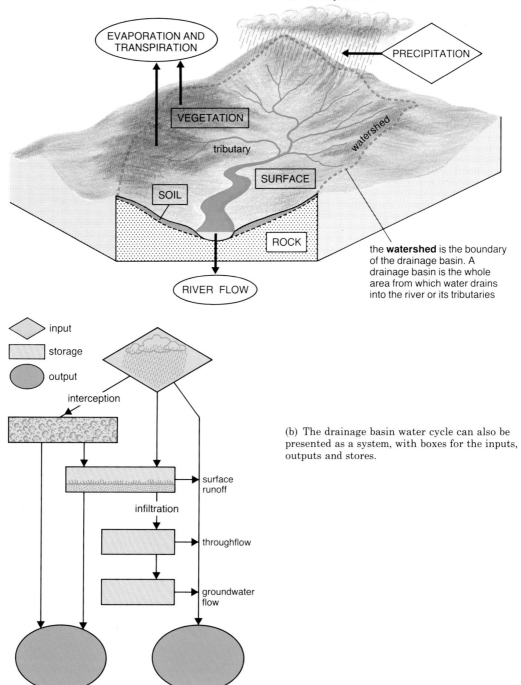

the **watershed** is the boundary of the drainage basin. A drainage basin is the whole area from which water drains into the river or its tributaries

(b) The drainage basin water cycle can also be presented as a system, with boxes for the inputs, outputs and stores.

Water storage

Rainwater which travels over land gets into the river very quickly. Water which gets held up in the storage zones may take days, weeks or even months to find its way into the river. If you think about it, that's why rivers don't dry up as soon as it stops raining! They are kept flowing by water seeping into them from the storage zones. One of the key processes affecting how much water can enter the storage zones is *infiltration*. Infiltration happens when rainwater soaks into the ground, and the infiltration rate measures how quickly water seeps into the soil. Carry out this simple experiment to see how quickly infiltration happens, and how the amount changes from place to place.

3 Cut out the top and bottom from a large tin (eg. a baked beans tin). Bury your tin to about half its depth in a well-dug piece of garden and pour 100 ml water into it. Make a note of the exact time the water takes to drain away. Repeat this experiment on different sorts of ground, for example part of a lawn, a sandpit, a well trampled piece of bare ground. It is also worth trying to do the experiment after a few dry days, and again after a day or two of heavy rain. Keep a careful note of all the drainage times taken. Write a short report to explain what seems to affect the speed of infiltration.

Table 2   Infiltration rates during a rain storm

Time from start (mins.)	0	5	10	15	20	25	30	35	40	45
Infiltration rate (mm/min.)	1.7	1.5	1.2	1.1	1	0.7	0.7	0.7	0.7	0.7

4 Draw a line graph to show the infiltration rate found in a longer experiment, where measurements were taken at one site for 45 minutes (Table 2). Use a scale of 1 cm to 5 mins on the horizontal, or X axis, and 1 cm to 0.5 mm per min on the vertical, or Y axis.
a) When is the infiltration rate highest?
b) What happens to the amount of infiltration as time goes on?

c) When rain is falling faster than it can soak into the soil, what happens to it?
d) If one storm comes quickly after another, what will happen to the amount of run-off in the second one?
e) Will the infiltration rate for concrete roads and pavements be high or low?

The last question hints at the fact that people can affect the amount of rainwater reaching the river, and the speed at which it gets there. The two main areas which we influence are the amount of vegetation, especially tree cover, and the amount of infiltration.

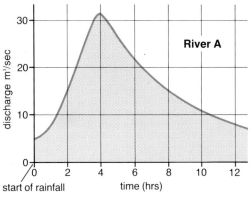
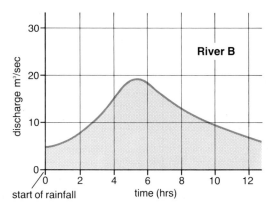

Figure 3.16 Hydrographs for two rivers showing the amount of water in the river at certain times after the start of the rain.

5 Figure 3.16 shows two graphs of the amount of water flowing in two rivers immediately after a rainstorm. The two rivers are very close together, of a similar size, and were affected by the same rainstorm. The only difference between the two drainage basins is that one is covered with coniferous forest, while the other only has grass cover.

By working through these questions you should be able to find out whether it is river A or river B which has a forested drainage basin. For each question answer river A or river B.
a) This river rises to its peak flow within 4 hours.
b) Water reaches this river more slowly.

c) More water must be stored on its way to this river.

d) There is less water in this river overall.

e) More water must be lost from this river's drainage basin from evaporation and transpiration.

The drainage basin described in parts b, c, d and e must be the forested one. More of the rainwater is caught on the leaves, and drips slowly to the ground giving it more time to infiltrate. Also a lot of the rainwater will probably be evaporated straight off the leaves.

So, afforestation of a catchment area will reduce river flow there. However, what will the effect be of building towns in a river catchment area? Think about what will happen to the infiltration rate. Remember also that drains, gutters and sewers will take rainwater speedily into the river, and that the places for storing water will be severely reduced.

6 Draw a flow diagram like Figure 3.15(b) to show the routes for rainwater through a heavily built-up area like the shopping centre of a city. You will probably need to use the following words:

drains   roads and pavements

surface run-off   sewers

evaporation   rainfall   roofs   gutters   river

It will help you to sketch a building with a roof and gutters first, then add a road with drains and sewers. Next decide which of the words given is the input, and which are the two outputs from the system. Now you can show the five storage places in the system, and name the flow or movement of water.

7 Figure 3.17 shows the river flow in a natural drainage basin. Imagine that most of this drainage basin is built on, as often happens when new towns like Harlow are built. Sketch what you think the graph of the river's flow would look like after a rain-storm, when the town was completely built.

Think about the differences in the items labelled on the diagram, such as time lag, peak discharge, rising limb. Label these differences on your own diagram.

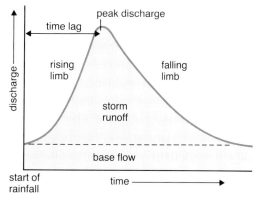

Figure 3.17 A typical storm hydrograph showing key terms.

River energy and work

The amount of water reaching the river, and flowing in it is very important, as it affects the amount of energy the river has to do work.

Figure 3.18 shows that a river's energy depends on the volume of the water, the speed of the water, and the height of the river above sea level. In simple terms we can say that this energy will be used first to overcome the friction of the bed and banks of the river, then to carry material, and finally to erode the bed and banks.

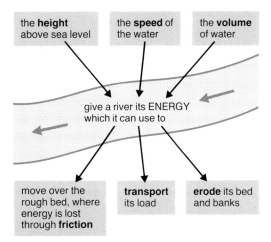

Figure 3.18 River energy – the sources of the energy and how it is used.

Figure 3.19(a) summarises the energy balance in a river system. You can see that if, for example, some extra water comes into the river, (Figure 3.19(b)), then to keep an energy balance there could be more transportation of material (Figure 3.19(c)).

In reality, it isn't easy to separate the uses of energy in a river like this. For instance, if a river is carrying tiny stones and silt particles, these will constantly be hitting the bed and banks of the river and eroding them. This is like constantly sandpapering the bed and banks, and think of the effect even very fine-grained sandpaper can have on wood.

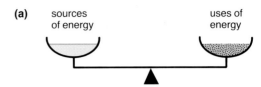

(a) sources of energy   uses of energy

The river has an **energy balance**

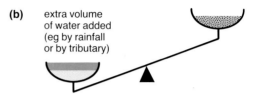

(b) extra volume of water added (eg by rainfall or by tributary)

If greater energy is available, the river must use more energy (do more work) to keep in balance

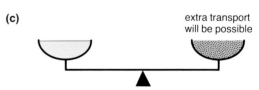

(c)   extra transport will be possible

The river uses up the extra energy by transporting or eroding. The balance is restored

Figure 3.19 The energy balance in a river system.

Exercise

1 Check you understand this idea of an energy balance by working out what effects the following changes could have on a river:

 a) A drought, which causes the river level to fall. (Remember that one or more of the uses of energy will also have to be reduced.)

 b) A section of the river bed is made much rougher, after concrete blocks are dumped in it.

 c) The river is straightened and given smooth concrete banks and a concrete bed as it passes through a village.

Figure 3.20 illustrates the way in which the river can transport material and erode its bed and banks.

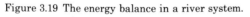

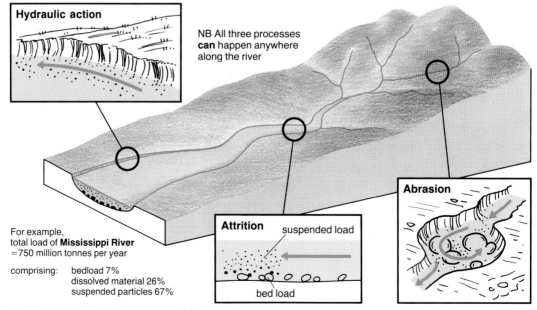

Hydraulic action

NB All three processes **can** happen anywhere along the river

For example, total load of **Mississippi River** = 750 million tonnes per year

comprising: bedload 7%
dissolved material 26%
suspended particles 67%

Attrition   suspended load

bed load

Abrasion

Figure 3.20 Some of the processes of river erosion.

When looking at the boulders lying on the bed of a river like the East Lyn, it is hard to imagine a river ever having enough force to move them. Figure 3.21 shows that it is indeed possible.

Figure 3.21 Boulders lie in the streets of Lynmouth after the 1952 flood.

2 Study Figure 3.20 then check your understanding of the following terms by matching the correct definition with each term. Write them out in pairs.

Term

Attrition
Abrasion
Hydraulic action
Suspended load
Dissolved load
Bed load

Definition

- The force of the water itself can be enough to dislodge earth from the bed and banks of the river.
- Particles of silt and tiny stones swirled round on the bed of the river grind away at the rock, and can create potholes.
- Some particles of mud, clay and sand are small enough to be carried permanently by the water.
- As the particles of suspended load hit one another and the bed load, they get broken up into smaller pieces which are easier to carry away.
- Large stones and boulders lying on the bed of the river will only be moved occasionally when the river is in flood.
- The river water will carry in it dissolved particles of soluble rocks such as chalk or limestone.

3 Estimate the volume (in cubic metres) of some of the boulders moved in the Lynmouth flood (Volume = length × width × depth). Use the size of people for scale – remembering that a person is roughly 1.5 m tall.

Features produced by rivers – some of the outputs of the system

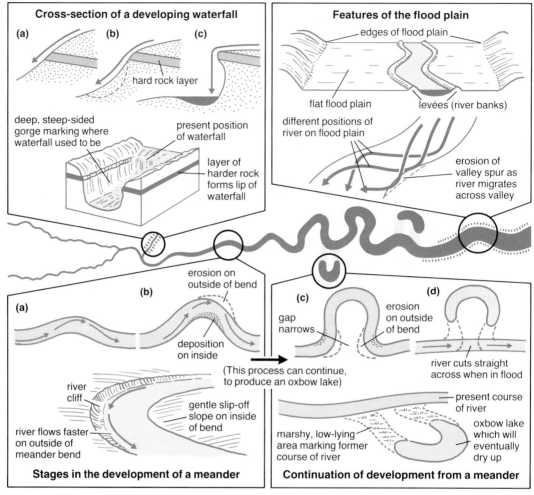

Figure 3.22 Some of the features you might expect to find along the course of a river.

The force of the river itself, together with the erosive power of its load, creates distinctive river features, such as those illustrated in Figure 3.22.

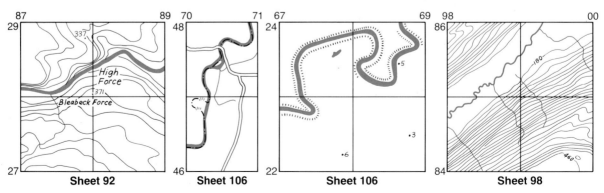

Figure 3.23 Four river features as shown on Ordnance Survey map extracts.

4 The O.S. map extracts in Figure 3.23 are of the same river features illustrated in Figure 3.22. Write a short description of the landscape shown on each map extract. Mention the actual heights, describe the steepness of slopes, indicate the river width and describe the appearance of the river and its valley. Decide which feature is shown on each extract, by comparing your description with Figure 3.22.

Deltas

A delta is a huge area of deposited mud, silt and clay which collects where the river water enters the sea (or a lake). As the water slows down on entering the sea, it drops its load, and this can gradually build up until it appears above the surface (Figure 3.24). As more and more silt, mud, sand and clay is deposited the river may find one route to the sea becomes blocked, so it breaks through in another direction. This branching produces *distributaries* which fan out over the delta. The build-up of sediment is helped by plants growing and trapping more mud, sand and silt. The plants also help to hold the delta sediments in place.

Exercise

1 Read through the following list of conditions and decide which ones would favour the formation of a delta at a river mouth:
   a) the river carries a huge load of mud, silt and clay;
   b) the sea rapidly becomes very deep off-shore, with a steep shelf;
   c) the sea has a very small tidal range;
   d) the sea is gentle, with few rough storms;
   e) plants are very slow to grow on the emerging sediment.

2 Two statements in Question 1 are incorrect. Re-write them correctly to show two more conditions which would help a delta to form.

Figure 3.24 Stages in the formation of a delta.

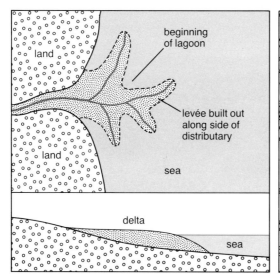
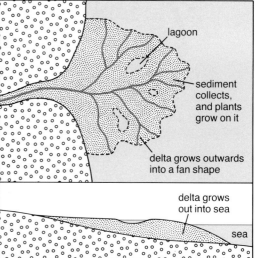

Deltas also form a link between the river system and the coastal system. Of course, deltas do not form at every river mouth, they will only form when the conditions are right.

Major deltas, like the Nile shown in Figure 3.25, are often very densely populated. This is because delta soils are very fertile, and every time the river floods, fresh deposits of alluvium are dropped. People are able to farm this land very intensively. The following study of Bangladesh illustrates the dangers of living in such an apparently attractive environment.

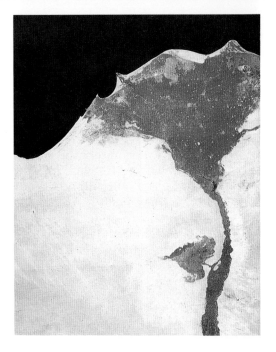

Figure 3.25 A satellite photograph of the Nile Delta. Notice the strip of fertile land beside the River Nile and how it contrasts with the desert on either side.

Bangladesh – a delta country

Bangladesh is a country which covers about the same area as England and Wales. However, it is very different in other ways. Most of Bangladesh is a flat alluvial plain, criss-crossed by many small rivers and canals, and three major rivers, the Ganges, the Brahmaputra and the Meghna. Together these form the largest delta in the world.

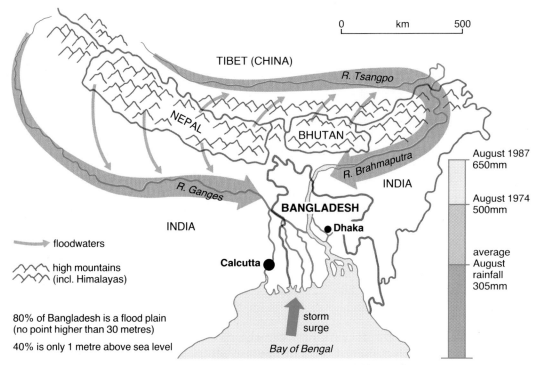

Figure 3.26 A diagram illustrating the build up to the Bangladesh flood disaster in 1987.

Figure 3.27 The Bangladesh flood disaster, 1988.

The whole delta plain is less than 30 m above sea level, with the average height less than 9 m. The average population density is 525 people per km², but densities reach 772 per km² along the river valleys. The Gross National Product (G.N.P.). per person gives an idea of the wealth produced by the people through industry, farming and services. For Bangladesh, the G.N.P. per person was £100 in 1986, compared with £5500 in the UK and £11 000 in the USA.

Three quarters of Bangladesh's annual rainfall (which averages 2500 mm) usually falls during their summer months of July, August and September. The summer rains are brought by the south west monsoon winds, which also cause intense storms along the coast. These storms drive the water in the Bay of Bengal up into huge waves which then crash on to the land.

Exercise

1 The background described above should help you to see why Bangladesh is likely to suffer floods. Pick four or more factors from the paragraphs above which suggest that flooding will be likely.

However, these background factors on their own do not necessarily cause flooding. We have to add to them some 'trigger' which sets the flood off. In fact, between 1960 and 1981 there were 17 flood events, which killed nearly 40 000 people. The worst flood events recently were in 1987 and 1988. In 1987 over 800 people died, over two million tonnes of grain were washed away, and three million tonnes of grain were destroyed. In 1988 the floods were even worse. Towards the end of August heavy rain and flooding rivers brought so much water to Bangladesh that more than half the country was flooded. In addition to the hundreds killed by flood water, many more died of diseases such as typhoid and cholera which spread rapidly as water supplies and sewage disposal were disrupted. Two major floods, one after the other — what will happen next year? Some say the floods will go on getting worse because the causes of flooding are not being prevented.

Some of the causes of flooding in Bangladesh are listed below.

- The Ganges river has been dammed in India, so that *less* water gets into Bangladesh in the dry season. The flow is lower, so more silt is dropped, blocking some of the river's channels.
- Deforestation (cutting down trees) in the Himalayas has caused massive soil erosion there (see page 134 for more details). The eroded soil gets into the rivers and fills up the river channels, meaning that the river can carry less water, and is therefore more likely to flood.
- The eroded soil carried by the rivers through Bangladesh is deposited on the flood plains in summer, building up the level of the land. Because land is so short in an overcrowded country, people then move onto this land to live. In this way, when a flood *does* come, more people are at risk.
- Many of the farming families live in houses built of wood and corrugated iron, which are easily destroyed by floods. People who lose their home find shelter in stoutly build concrete schools and community centres.
- Bangladesh's rivers flow into a fairly narrow bay, the Bay of Bengal, where a high tide, or even worse, a tidal surge, can stop the rivers' water flowing out to sea.
- The August rainfall was higher than normal in 1987 and 1988.

2 Which of these is the main 'trigger' which set off the recent floods?

3 Which of these factors are outside the control of the Bangladesh Government?

4 Can anything be done to prevent these factors contributing together to make a disastrous flood?

5 Why do people continue to move onto the river flood plain, in spite of the known danger?

Rivers and their basins as a resource

Figure 3.28 shows just a few of the ways in which rivers prove useful to us. How many can you list? Two uses are outlined below.

Reservoir construction

One of the most obvious benefits of rivers is to create reservoirs by building dams across them. Reservoirs might be built to provide a water supply for domestic and industrial use, or alternatively they may be built to supply irrigation water in drought-prone countries. They are sometimes also used for hydro-electric power generation. Whatever the reason for building them, reservoirs make huge changes to the river landscape, as shown in Figure 3.30 (page 54).

Tourism

There is often a conflict between the needs of a country's tourist industry, and its water supply requirements. Figure 3.33 on page 55 shows some of the effects that building the Aswan dam had in Egypt. How many unwelcome effects can you find? What are they?

Figure 3.28 Some of the many uses to which rivers can be put.

Figure 3.29 A cruise ship on the River Nile.

Exercise

1 a) What opposition do you think there might be to a proposal to create the reservoir in Figure 3.30, and from whom would the opposition come?

b) Can you think of any local people who might be keen to see the reservoir built?

c) Reservoirs like this are built by Water Authorities. Why do they build them?

Who will use the water stored in them? Are these users likely to be local?

d) Will the construction of the dam and reservoir have any effect on river erosion below the dam? Explain your answer carefully. (The information on river flows on page 46 may help you.)

Figure 3.30 The effects of dam construction and the creation of a reservoir on a valley.

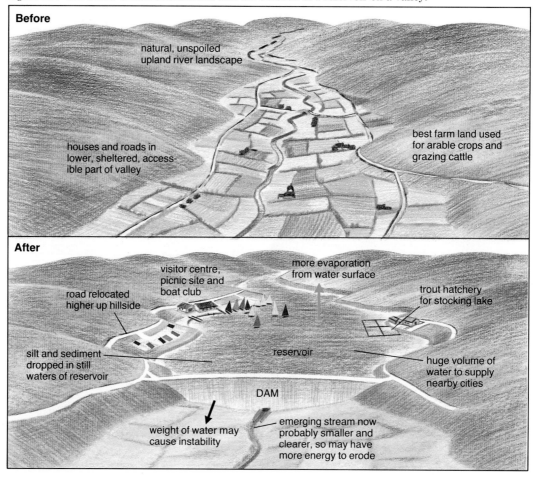

Nile Cruises

2 Look at the extract from the newspaper article from January 1988 about Nile cruises (Figure 3.31). The area described is shown in the map in Figure 3.32 and the photograph in Figure 3.29 on page 53.

a) What problem is described in the extract?

b) What reason is given for the problem?

c) Why has the building of the Aswan dam also contributed to the problem? (Think about what happens to rainwater entering the Nile above the dam.)

d) Why are boats allowed through the Esna lock only at certain times of the day? (Find out how locks work; you could draw diagrams as part of your answer).

e) Why is the Egyptian government keen to keep the Nile cruises going? (Remember this is a relatively poor country).

Despite putting on a brave face, tour operators with thousands of bookings for Nile cruises over the next year are having to make last-minute changes to itineraries. In the past three months, passengers, some paying up to £2,500, have had to resort to coaches and aircraft to visit sights because their cruises have been cut short or diverted. One Nile trip has been brought forward by two months to make the most of the higher water levels in summer.

The disruption is caused by eight successive years of drought in the Ethiopian Highlands. Rain from the mountains ultimately feeds the Nile and without it the river is drying up. There is no sign that the situation will improve.

With the water level low, however, some tour operators find it difficult to meet their schedules. Some ships, usually the older ones with deep keels, cannot get far north of Luxor and so cannot sail either down to Luxor from Cairo or up to the capital from Aswan.

But the biggest problem is a lock at Esna. This has to be navigated to get between Aswan and Luxor, and since the beginning of this month the Egyptian ministry of irrigation is allowing ships through it only at certain times of the day. The result is a bottleneck.

Some vessels still cannot manage it. Hotel boats owned by Hilton International, for example, have been unable to pass through the lock. To make sure cruises are not cut short, two of these ships have to meet either side of the lock and passengers from each vessel switch cabins to continue their trips.

Many bigger tour operators such as Kuoni Travel, Thomson Worldwide, and Thomas Cook Faraway Holidays appear fairly confident. They say their cruises have hardly been affected.

Other tour operators were blunt about their fears. Brian Swan-Taylor, general manager for Swan Hellenic, said: "We have to operate with our fingers crossed."

The company — one of the leading operators on the Nile — has dropped its 600-mile trips from Aswan to Cairo or Cairo to Aswan. Instead, it is only running cruises from Aswan to north of Luxor and back again.

Figure 3.31 'Where the river is running dry' – the case of the disappearing Nile!
The Sunday Times 31.1.88 © Edward Welch

Figure 3.32 The location of the River Nile.

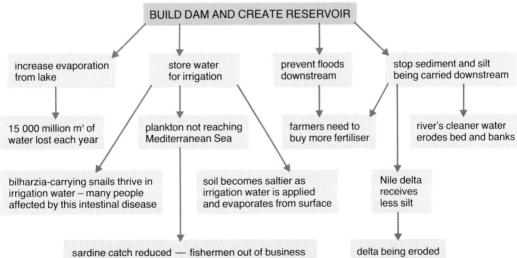

Figure 3.33 A flow diagram which illustrates some of the consequences, deliberate and otherwise, of building the Aswan Dam across the River Nile.

Changes in rivers

The Mississippi, USA

Rivers are always changing their courses as part of their natural development. However, people have an important part to play in this area, too. For example, the Mississippi river has changed its course several times in the last five thousand years. As its delta has built up, making the river's route into the sea more gentle and more likely to be clogged up by silt, the river has occasionally broken through and found a new way into the sea. The old river course is abandoned and a new delta forms. (Figure 3.34.) Unfortunately such a change would not be very popular today, because the river is used for a huge amount of transport, and has two very important ports built on it – Baton Rouge and New Orleans.

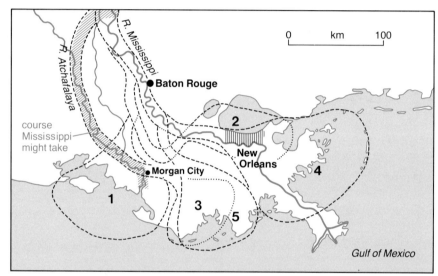

Figure 3.34 Previous positions of the Mississippi Delta. The Mississippi Delta, USA

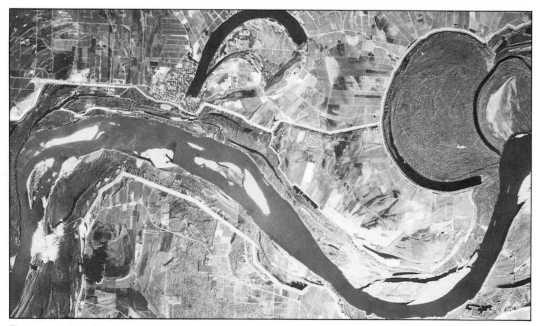

Figure 3.35 Aerial photograph of the Mississippi River.

There have been fears in recent years that the Mississippi might pour out of its present channel into the bed of the Atchafalaya river, at a point about 300 km from New Orleans. The reason for the breakthrough would be to give the river a new, steeper, more direct route into the sea. A series of barrages has already been built to prevent too much of the Mississippi's water running into the Atchafalaya, but these are being eroded. Not only would Baton Rouge and New Orleans be left high and dry by such a dramatic change, but the new river would cut a path straight through some of the state's best farmland, and across pipelines carrying natural gas inland from the offshore fields! No wonder the Mississippi is now virtually a canal in its later stages, and is no longer allowed to go where it likes.

Closer to home, there are rivers in Britain whose courses are also changing. We often use rivers as boundaries, sometimes of parishes, and more often of farmers' land. Looking at Figure 3.36, think about what would happen if a river meander is cut off, and the river's new course straightened out.

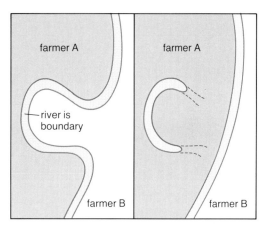

Figure 3.36 Changes in land ownership which can result when a river changes its course, by cutting off a meander bend.

The River Bollin, Cheshire

Six meander cut offs on the River Bollin between 1935 and 1973 meant that the farmer in Bollin House Farm made a net gain of 0.7 ha of land. Much of this extra land is poor quality though, consisting of oxbow lake, marsh, scrub and weed covered land.

Figure 3.37 shows part of the River Bollin where this happened. This river has recently changed its course several times, and in fact a meander was observed being cut off in July 1973. This particular meander had a neck width of 70 m in 1872, but the rate of narrowing was only 0.14 m/year between 1872 and 1935. It was in the period 1935–73 that the fastest erosion happened, and the width of the meander neck decreased by 1.73 m per year. In that same 38 year period there were no fewer than seven meander cut offs.

This extra erosion happened because the river has more energy, which in turn is the result of extra water in the river. But why has the river's flow increased? The rainfall has not increased, so instead more of the existing rain water must be getting into the river quickly. Thinking back to page 45 we know that a change in infiltration could be one possible reason. In this example, infiltration has decreased because of the building of new urban areas at Macclesfield, Prestbury and Wilmslow. There are more concrete surfaces, more storm sewers and more drains to take water rapidly into the river. The second reason why more rain water reaches the river is that much of the surrounding farm land was tile drained – tile drains are like pipes which are laid deep beneath the soil to carry water quickly away from the soil as it infiltrates.

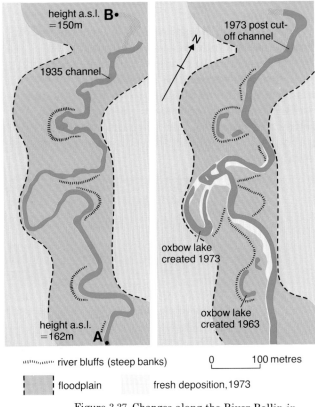

river bluffs (steep banks)

floodplain   fresh deposition, 1973

0   100 metres

Figure 3.37 Changes along the River Bollin in Cheshire over the last 50 years.

Exercise

1 Use Figure 3.37 to draw a map showing the old route of the River Bollin before the cut offs happened. Measure the original length of the river, and its length today without the bends.
   a) What has happened to the total length of river since 1935?
   b) The drop in height of the river from A to B is still the same, so what has happened to its gradient, the slope? To find out, sketch a triangle like the one in Figure 3.38 to show the old river slope. Mark in the height drop from A to B in metres, and the length of the river in 1935 in metres. Use these figures to work out the gradient. Then sketch a second triangle and mark in the new river length, and the same height drop as before. What is the gradient now? How has it changed?

2 a) Fortunately, there are no road bridges on this part of the River Bollin. If there were, what danger might they be in?
   b) If permission is given for a new village or town to be built in the countryside, what could the Local Water Authority do to prevent similar river changes happening? Who do you think should pay for any work that might be needed?

Reducing the flood hazard

It is natural for rivers to flood, as we saw on page 51, and in fact floods have been very valuable in creating alluvial flood plains and deltas which provide farmers with very fertile soil. It is also true that floods are recorded as the most frequently occurring disaster, and that floods were the cause of 200 000 deaths worldwide between 1947 and 1981. Although the hazard has been ever present for centuries, the disastrous effects of floods have increased as the population of the world has grown, and more people live on and farm these very fertile areas. There are several ways in which we can try to reduce the flood hazard.

a) *Deliberate channel changes*

A river which meanders at great length over a low lying area will cause much more severe flooding than a straighter river with a slightly steeper gradient. Therefore some flood prevention schemes involve cutting new straighter diversions for rivers, either by making a completely new channel or by cutting off some meander bends. A good example in Britain is found in East Anglia (see Figure 3.39) where, in the seventeenth century, two channels 34 km long were built to carry the River Ouse more quickly to the sea. Entrance to these two channels is controlled by a sluice gate, so that when the river becomes very full, more of it

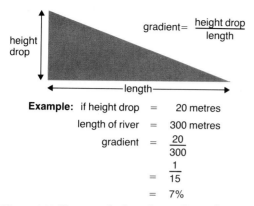

Example: if height drop = 20 metres

length of river = 300 metres

gradient = $\dfrac{20}{300}$

= $\dfrac{1}{15}$

= 7%

Figure 3.38 How to calculate the gradient of a river.

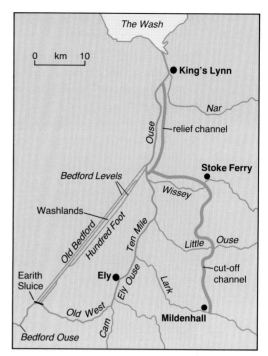

Figure 3.39 A map showing the scheme to reduce flooding on the Great Ouse River.

can be diverted along the cuts. In winter the washlands between the channels are deliberately flooded to store the water temporarily. These washlands are a very important wildlife habitat.

b) *Embankments, levees and flood barriers*

Embankments are a relatively cheap and easy means to confine a river and prevent it flooding the surrounding land. Embankments were built beside the Thames in London between 1869 and 1874 to protect the city. However, since then it has been shown that the city needs more protection. One event which made this very clear was the severe flooding on the East Coast in 1953.

These floods were caused by a tidal surge in the North Sea. A deep depression moved eastwards over Britain and the North Sea. The wind was blowing strongly from the north, forcing water southwards in the North Sea. In the south of the North Sea, water is funnelled through a narrow gap – the English channel – and its level builds up as it cannot force its way through. Some water pours up estuaries like the River Thames. If a storm surge happens at the same time as a high spring tide, disaster strikes. The 1953 flood affected the coast of Britain from Scotland to Kent. 307 people died, and 32 000 had to be evacuated. About 24 000 homes were destroyed and about 480 km^2 of land were submerged and damaged by salt.

London itself suffered some flooding, and so, because the threat of flooding in general was increasing, it was finally decided to build a flood barrier across the Thames. The threat of flooding is increasing for several reasons:

i)   mean sea level in South East England is rising at a rate of about 30 cm every 100 years;

ii) central London is steadily sinking because of the weight of buildings on the clay;

iii) as more building takes place, impervious surfaces replace porous soils, so less rainwater is stored in the earth, and more gets quickly into the river.

The Thames flood barrier

Construction of the Thames flood barrier (Figure 3.40) began in 1973 and it was finished in 1982. It was estimated that it would only be needed once or twice a year this century, and that by the year 2030 it might be necessary to close it ten times a year.

Figure 3.40 The Thames Barrier from the north bank of the river.

The site at Woolwich was chosen for three main reasons. Firstly, there are suitable chalk foundations there. Secondly, because it is in the middle of a long straight reach of river, shipping has good warning that it is approaching. Thirdly, since the docks upstream are closing or have been closed, less water traffic needs to get past the barrier.

There are six navigation gates, four of them 60 m wide and two 30 m wide. Each gateway has a rising sector gate which can rotate into different positions – four of them are shown in Figure 3.41. The gates are normally in position (1). When there is a high spring tide which needs holding back, the gate is put first in position (2) and then into position (4). It then allows *some* water up river to give a normal tide-rise upstream. Position (3) is used for cleaning and repairing the gate.

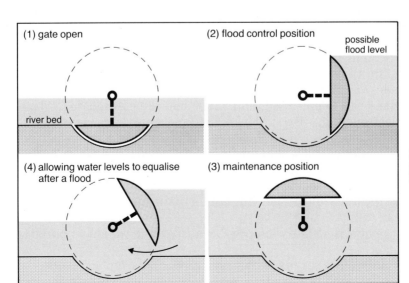

Figure 3.41 The four gate positions of the Thames Barrier.

Of course, this barrier would be of little use without river walls on the down-stream side of it. These river walls protect the lower part of the estuary from floods when the barrier is across the river.

The city of Hull has also built a flood barrier across the mouth of the River Hull where it joins the Humber. It is a much smaller structure as it protects a much narrower river, and works like a guillotine, dropping down into the river and holding back the water behind it.

In addition to deliberate channel changes and embankments, there are three further methods of reducing the flood hazard

c) *Flood storage reservoirs*

Reservoirs in Britain have never been built just as a means of flood storage, but some reservoirs do have this as an additional reason for having been built. Of course, such reservoirs cannot be built on the lowland rivers of Britain because there are no, or very few, suitable sites. If the land is all low-lying, a dam cannot be built to trap water behind it, as it can across a deep narrow valley. So it is not usually possible to build storage dams across these lowland rivers, which are the ones most likely to have floods on them.

d) *Flood plain zoning*

This involves designating areas of the flood plain which are likely to be flooded as unsuitable for building. Planners and Water Authorities must therefore discuss the flood hazard, so that planners can then prevent development in the hazardous areas. This strategy has not been used much in Britain. In fact much housing has been built in, for example, Maidenhead, Oxford, Reading and Windsor on land that was flooded by the Thames in 1947.

Exercise

1 Figure 3.42 shows the built-up area of Nottingham, and the flood plain of the River Trent.
   a) Estimate the percentage of the River Trent's flood plain which has been built on.

   b) What do you notice about the earliest building of this city and its suburbs?
   c) Has there been any change in decisions to build on the flood plain over time? Explain your answer.

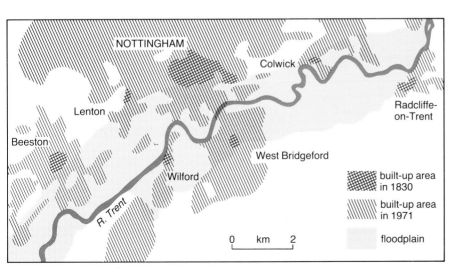

Figure 3.42 The growth of housing on and near the Trent flood plain in Nottingham.

e) *Flood forecasting and warning schemes*

With better weather forecasting and with models to look at the effect of rainfall on rivers, it ought to be possible to warn people of the risk of a flood before it happens. Emergency services can then be on standby, sandbags distributed and people ready to evacuate their homes. This may prevent loss of life, but will do little to reduce damage to property. Shrewsbury, on the River Severn is Shropshire, has such a flood warning plan, including a clear network of people to spread the message from one to another.

Wetlands

Wetlands in Britain, such as the Norfolk Broads and the Somerset Levels, suffer from being neither land nor water; people always want to 'improve' them. 'Land is all right; you can live on it and walk or drive on it and build on it. Water is all right because you can sail a boat on it and move from one place to another. But wetlands mostly are neither one nor the other.'

Our wetlands are under threat. Some, such as the Norfolk Broads, are under threat from tourists, while others are threatened by farmers who wish to drain them for agriculture. Remember, this is in a country which already contributes huge food surpluses to various food mountains. However, the conservation of these wetlands is now becoming a priority.

The Norfolk Broads

The Broads are the remains of ancient peat diggings which were flooded by a rise in the sea level in the Middle Ages. They lie along the rivers Ant, Bure, Thurne, Chet, Yare and Waveney, and form a very distinctive landscape. The fact that they are now under threat has led people to consider how to protect them. But first, there are four problem areas to consider.

a) *Water quality*

Figure 3.43(a) shows the water quality in the Norfolk Broads. The water quality is divided into three phases.

To move more of the Broads from phase 3 into phases 1 and 2, several things are being done.

- Water quality is monitored very carefully so that discharges of nutrient-rich water are not allowed.
- Farmers are being given advice and financial help to dispose of slurry with care.
- Phosphate-rich mud is being pumped out of the dykes and rivers.
- Zooplankton are being introduced into the rivers, because they feed on algae.
- Phosphate removal plants are being set up at sewage works.

b) *Bank erosion*

In some places the river banks have been eroded up to 3 m in ten years. Why has this happened?

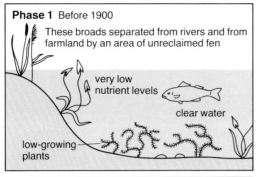

Phase 1 Before 1900

These broads separated from rivers and from farmland by an area of unreclaimed fen

very low nutrient levels

clear water

low-growing plants

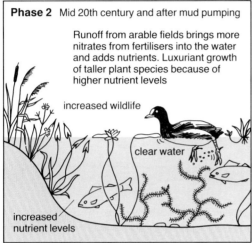

Phase 2 Mid 20th century and after mud pumping

Runoff from arable fields brings more nitrates from fertilisers into the water and adds nutrients. Luxuriant growth of taller plant species because of higher nutrient levels

increased wildlife

clear water

increased nutrient levels

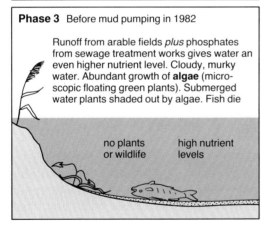

Phase 3 Before mud pumping in 1982

Runoff from arable fields *plus* phosphates from sewage treatment works gives water an even higher nutrient level. Cloudy, murky water. Abundant growth of **algae** (microscopic floating green plants). Submerged water plants shaded out by algae. Fish die

no plants or wildlife

high nutrient levels

Figure 3.43(a) The three phases of water quality identified in the Norfolk Broads.

Banks can be protected naturally and artificially using the following methods.

- If the bank is altered to a more gentle slope, plants can be encouraged to re-colonise it. This will only work if the water quality is improved. Boats must also be kept away from the banks as their wash would prevent the plants re-colonising.
- Steel piling can be driven in to the water's edge, so that it protects the banks. This looks ugly, and prevents plants and animals from living in and along the riverbank.
- A new bank profile can be made using rolls of Enkamat, a nylon mesh inlaid with asphalt, laid on top of peat. Reeds and other plants hold the bank in place with their roots. Although artificial, this bank protection is more environmentally acceptable.

(a) Section through a river bank before the Broads had high motor boat use and water quality problems

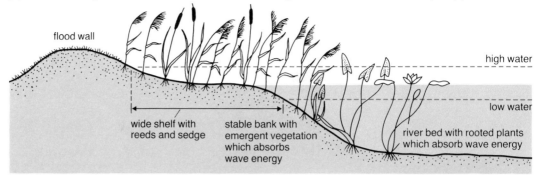

(b) Section through a river bank suffering bank erosion

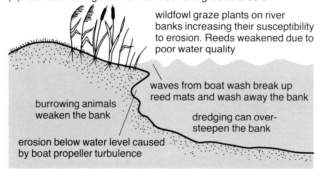

(c) Section through a river bank protected by sheet steel piling

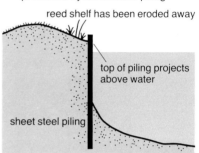

Figure 3.43(b) Bank erosion and its prevention along rivers of the Norfolk Broads.

Exercise

Look at Figure 3.43(b).

1 Describe the main difference between the river bank before and after it started suffering erosion.

2 Pick out two causes of erosion which are caused by the use of the Broads for holiday motor boats.

3 In what way does the poor water quality help to encourage bank erosion?

- Boats are being designed to produce less of a wash. Long, thin boats tend to be better at this, and the slower a boat travels the less wash is created.

c) *The problems of tourism*

The Broads are used for boating holidays, using the 1800 boats available for weekly hire. There are also some passenger boats, and some boats available for day hire. The Broads are also used for fishing, both from boats and from the riverbanks. The main problems related to recreational use of the Broads are:
- Congestion – either because of overcrowding or because of bottlenecks occurring, for example at a narrow bridge.
- Conflicts of use between different groups such as boat hirers, anglers, waterskiers and sailors.

What can be done to prevent these conflicts of use?

Areas could be zoned for one activity, perhaps at particular times of the day. People can also be made more aware of the needs of different groups, so that, for example, boat hirers keep well away from an angler's line.

The arrival of so many tourists has meant that kiosks and amusement halls have sprung up, spoiling the very scenery people came to see. There are also chalets and houseboats lining some of the river banks. All of this tourist development will now be controlled, and new facilities like toilets and visitor centres will be provided.

Figure 3.44 The Norfolk Broads.

d) *Draining marshland for agriculture*

The Halvergate Marshes cover about 5500 hectares between the River Bure and the River Yare. The marshland is crossed by a network of drainage ditches, and water from these ditches is pumped up into the embanked rivers. In summer, the water table is low enough for cattle and horses to be grazed. In winter fewer animals can be grazed, but many birds arrive to spend the winter there. A rich variety of flowers and plants has also developed on the marshland.

Deep drainage and ploughing for cereals or ley grass would ruin this habitat, as both fertiliser and pesticide would have to be used. Instead, farmers are being encouraged to conserve the marshes, keeping the permanent grassland, and following conservation scheme guidelines for grazing (see Figure 3.45). Farmers who have agreed to join the scheme are paid £50 per acre (£123.55 per ha) each year for three years to compensate them for lack of cereal income.

Without any intervention these problems would cause a rapid change in the environment. To prevent this deterioration there is a Broads authority, and the Broads are to be protected as a National Park.

Exercise

1 Look at all four problem areas and for each one summarise what would happen to the Broads if there were no management plan for it.

These guidelines summarise the main provisions of the scheme. If you join you must agree not to plough or destroy the sward on the land included in the scheme and to follow these management guidelines:

(a) Graze with cattle, sheep or horses.

(b) Keep an average stocking rate on the marshes within the range 0.5–1.5 livestock units per acre during the grazing season, i.e. approximately one mature beast or six sheep to the acre. Day to day stocking levels can be freely adjusted to take account of differences in land quality, stock and grassland management, weather conditions or veterinary necessity.

(c) Take no more than a single cut of hay or silage each year and graze the aftermath.

(d) Consult the Broads Grazing Scheme Unit for further advice *before* considering:

– removing any landscape or archaeological features (such as trees, reedbeds, dykes);

– erecting any buildings or constructing roads;

– improving any grazing marshes by under-drainage, levelling, or direct seeding;

– applying more than 100 units of nitrogen per acre;

– applying any herbicide, other than the use of simple MCPA or mecoprop against thistles, docks or ragwort.

Figure 3.45 Grazing guidelines produced by the Broads Grazing Marshes Conservation Scheme.

2 Look at the sketches of the eight people who are interested in the future of the Broads (Figure 3.46). Pick out pairs of people who you think will have similar views about this. Now pick out pairs of people who might oppose one another. Why do you think they are in opposition?

3 There are several ways of controlling and improving the situation in the Broads. Pick out from the four sections above the controls and measures that would be very expensive to put into operation, and list them. Then list all the changes that could happen relatively cheaply.

4 Whose responsibility are the changes? Should they be paid for by:
   a) the boat hirers through their hire boat companies?
   b) the local people through their rates?
   c) the Government – which really means all of us through our taxes?

Decide who you think should pay, and give some reasons for your answer.

biology teacher at local school

tourist in cabin cruiser

owner of shop in Wroxham

owner of boatyard

Friends of the Earth

local retiree with yacht

farmer

RSPB birdwatcher

Figure 3.46 Some of the people who are concerned about future developments in the Broads.

Somerset Levels

This is another area of low lying marshland, criss-crossed by dykes, and originally used for summer pasture. The flow diagram in Figure 3.47 shows what has happened to the area as farmers have installed diesel pumps to drain the land more efficiently.

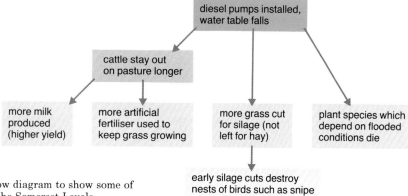

Figure 3.47 A simple flow diagram to show some of the effects of draining the Somerset Levels.

Exercise

1 To reverse the damage, the water table needs to be allowed to rise. Imagine that this happens, and work out from Figure 3.47 what the effect will be on:
a) milk yield;
b) the use of fertiliser;
c) the cutting of grass for silage;
d) nesting birds;
e) plant species.
Why would farmers have to be paid to undertake such conservation measures?

The Coastal System

In the river system, water and land interact to produce a set of distinctive features. The coastal system operates in the same way, but in this case the water is the sea, constantly washing against the strip of land which marks the coast. The power of the sea to alter the land comes from its speed and volume, as the river's energy did. The sea also uses the material that it picks up and carries to help it erode the rocks of the coast.

The force of sea water at the coast is shown in the waves which break on the beach or cliff. These waves start far out to sea, and are created and driven by the wind. The longer the distance waves travel over, the larger they are. The distance they have travelled over is called the *fetch* of the wave.

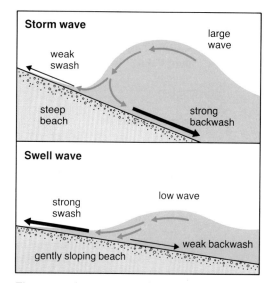

Figure 3.48 A comparison of two sorts of breaking waves – storm waves and swell waves.

In fact it is the wave that is travelling, not the water. If you watch a ball bobbing about on the waves you see that the ball goes up and down as the wave passes. The water only moves forwards when the wave breaks. The wave breaks when the depth of water is less than the depth of the wave (Figure 3.48). As the wave breaks some water washes up the beach and then falls back down again.

Sometimes large, high waves break almost vertically onto the beach. These are called *storm waves*. There is a strong pull of water down the beach, and material is carried down with the water. These destructive waves can erode the beach, by carrying material away. Such storm waves might also throw shingle high up the beach, creating a *storm ridge*, with a steep slope down to the sea (Figure 3.49).

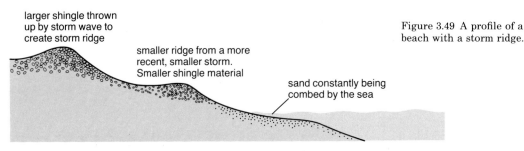

larger shingle thrown up by storm wave to create storm ridge

smaller ridge from a more recent, smaller storm. Smaller shingle material

sand constantly being combed by the sea

Figure 3.49 A profile of a beach with a storm ridge.

A shallower wave, called a *swell wave*, may spill on to the beach, and the main force of water is up the beach. These waves can build the beach up. Steep, storm waves are produced when the wind is blowing on-shore – this is the *dominant wind*. The *prevailing wind* is the one which blows most often. If the prevailing wind is also the dominant wind, the coast will be subjected to very erosive waves.

Wave fetch and wind frequency in Cornwall and East Yorkshire

Exercise

Use Table 3 to draw a wind rose, showing the frequency with which the wind blows from different directions at Gwennap Head in Cornwall and Spurn Point in Humberside.

Table 3

Direction	N	NE	E	SE	S	SW	W	NW
Spurn Point								
Frequency in days	13	31	39	28	71	60	74	26
Gwennap Head								
Frequency in days	35	34	36	11	27	102	71	41

To draw a wind rose, you need to draw a graph outline like the one in Figure 3.50(a). Use a scale of approximately 1 cm to 20 days. Use the same scale for both wind roses.

Now draw two histograms showing the frequency with which the wind blows at different speeds (Table 4). A histogram is a special type of graph which has frequency marked on the vertical axis, as in Figure 3.50(b).

Table 4

Wind speed (knots)	Days	
	Gwennap Head	Spurn Point
0	8	23
1–10	84	125
11–21	167	168
22–33	78	47
>34	28	2

Finally use an Atlas to work out the length of fetch in the relevant directions at each place (Table 5).

Table 5

	Gwennap Head	Spurn Point
NW	260 km	N/A
W	4000 km	N/A
SW		N/A
S		
SE		
E		450 km
NE	N/A	650 km
N	N/A	

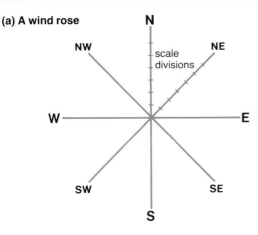

(a) A wind rose

scale divisions

N
NW   NE
W   E
SW   SE
S

(b) A histogram

frequency (number of days)

180
160
140
120
100
80
60
40
20
0

0   1–10 11-20 21-30 >31
wind speed (knots)

Figure 3.50(a) Outline for the construction of a wind rose to show the frequency with which the wind blows from different directions.

(b) Framework for a histogram showing the frequency of winds of different strengths.

Now use all your graphs and tables to answer these questions:
a) What is the prevailing wind at each place? Is it also the dominant (on-shore) wind at each place?

b) At which place do the waves have the greatest fetch?
c) At which place are the waves likely to be strongest? Give evidence for your answer.

The waves hitting the cliffs and beach have power to erode, partly through the force of the water itself. The waves also *abrade* cliffs by throwing shingle at them, giving the same sand-papering effect that rivers have on the land. The beach is a buffer between the waves and the cliff. If the beach is wide, the waves may never, or very seldom, attack the cliffs behind. Instead all the wave's energy is used up in moving beach material around.

Cliff erosion

Where waves attack the sea cliffs, their erosive effect is concentrated at the bottom of the cliff, so that a *wave cut notch* may be produced there. If this erosion continues in one area, the upper part of the cliff face may eventually collapse, so that the whole cliff face has retreated. The broken and shattered rock fragments

Figure 3.51 Granite cliffs at Land's End in Cornwall.

will form beach material. Particular areas of weakness in the rock like joints or faults will be eroded more easily than the surrounding rocks.

With no erosion at the base of the cliff a *scree* would probably build up. A scree is an irregular heap of weathered rock fragments which fall from the cliff and collect at the bottom of the cliff. The scree will gradually build up and cover the bare rock face. Some of Britain's most spectacular cliffs occur in very hard rocks which can support very steep slopes because of their great strength. The photograph in Figure 3.53 shows some examples.

Britain's cliffs have several uses: they give us dramatic scenery; they provide habitats for plants and sea birds; the material from them is often an important ingredient in supplying beaches further along the coast. But many of these cliffs are under threat because of human activity. Figure 3.54 suggests why.

Exercise

1 Look at Figure 3.53 which shows some features of coastal erosion. The three features shown form a sequence. In which order would they form – ie. which comes first; how would the first develop into the second, and so on.

2 Cliffs are formed wherever the slope is being actively eroded at the base – in this case by the sea. Look at Figure 3.52 and describe the appearance of the wave cut notch. Why does it form there?

3 What happens to the material that falls from the eroded cliff face?

4 What would happen to the shape of the cliff if the sea no longer eroded the base of the cliff? Look back to the section on mass wasting on page 36 to help you here.

5 Draw a sketch of Figure 3.53 to show the main coastal features. Begin by drawing a box the same size as the photograph. Then draw in the main outline of the land and sea. Next, put in some shading lines to show the

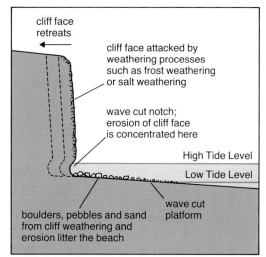

Figure 3.52 The processes involved in the formation of a cliff.

slope and some details of the cliff face. Finally label your sketch as fully as you can.

6 Is it fair to say that tourists ruin the very scenery they come to enjoy? Can anything be done to prevent this happening?

Figure 3.53 Coastal erosion features at Old Harry Rocks on the Dorset coast.

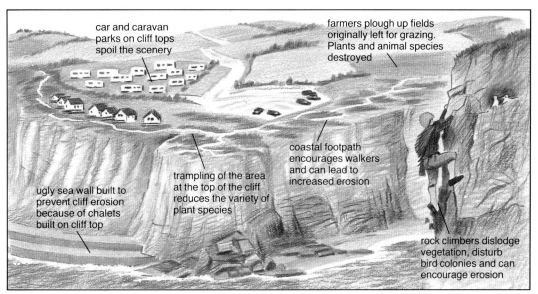

car and caravan
parks on cliff tops
spoil the scenery

farmers plough up fields
originally left for grazing.
Plants and animal species
destroyed

coastal footpath
encourages walkers
and can lead to
increased erosion

ugly sea wall built to
prevent cliff erosion
because of chalets
built on cliff top

trampling of the area
at the top of the cliff
reduces the variety of
plant species

rock climbers dislodge
vegetation, disturb
bird colonies and can
encourage erosion

Figure 3.54 Human threats to a sea cliff.

Beaches

Waves do not just erode. They also transport material and deposit it. If you imagine a beach, you probably visualise rounded pebbles, shingle and sand. They are rounded and broken down by the sea constantly washing them together and against cliffs. As waves break, they wash material up the shore. From there some of it might be carried back towards the sea by the backwash. Large storm waves can throw beach material well up the beach to form a ridge. This beach material is often larger than that lower down near the sea's edge. (See Figure 3.49).

If the waves break at an angle to the coast, then shingle and sand will also be moved at an angle up the beach, with the swash. The backwash from the wave will run back down the slope of the beach by the shortest route into the sea, ie. straight back to the sea.

If you imagine this happening over and over again you can see that individual pebbles and sand grains will gradually be moved along the beach. This process of movement along the beach is called *longshore drift*. The direction in which it happens is affected by the wind direction. In Figure 3.55(a) the wind is south-westerly, driving the waves on shore at an angle, and moving shingle from west to east along the beach.

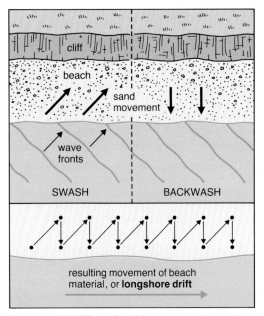

Figure 3.55(a) Waves breaking at an angle on the beach will sweep sand and shingle along the beach. This process is called *longshore drift*.

If longshore drift continues in the same direction and nothing is done to stop it, gradually all the beach material will move along the coast. This could mean that the beach at a seaside resort is gradually taken away to somewhere further along the coast. To prevent this happening *groynes* are built. Groynes are fences, often made of wood, which are built out from the back of the beach to the sea. They trap any sand which is moved along the beach. This often means that sand and shingle are built up high on one side of the groyne, but are much lower on the other side. (Figure 3.55(b).)

When sand is able to move along the coast unchecked it may form features called *spits*. Imagine a piece of coastline which turns a fairly sharp corner, as in Figure 3.56. As sand and shingle reach the 'corner' they will start to build up under water, forming an invisible extension to the land. Eventually enough sand or shingle will collect for the spit to emerge above the water, and it will slowly grow outwards from the land. The end of the spit is often curved by waves approaching from different directions.

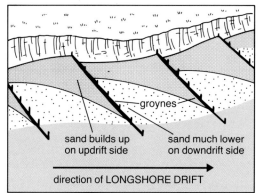

Figure 3.55(b) Sand will build up on the downdrift side of groynes. These are wooden fences built down the beach to trap the sand and prevent it being carried right away by longshore drift.

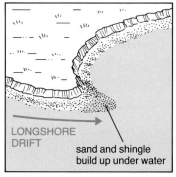
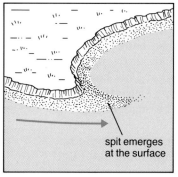
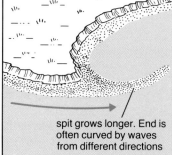

Figure 3.56 Three stages in the formation of a spit.

Spurn Head and Orford Ness

Spits have several effects on the physical and human landscape. Look at Figures 3.57–3.59 which show two famous spits.

Spurn Head was breached in 1850 in several places. That date marked the time for Spurn to be destroyed and re-formed. The situation was probably not helped by the removal of 50 000 tons of cobbles and gravel from its beaches each year in the 1840s. However, in 1850, the breaches were mended. So Spurn has been held artificially in its present position for the last 130 years. It has been breached recently though, in 1976 and again in 1988. It no longer has any protection from the coast to the north of it because the coast has been so severely eroded.

Exercise

1 What effects has Orford Ness had on its local area, particularly the River Alde? Try to explain the effect it has had.

2 How far is Spurn Head from Hull?

3 Why was it a good site for a lifeboat station and a coastguard lookout?

4 What is the main danger to the people who live on Spurn Head?

5 Who finds it important to keep Spurn Head intact, protecting it from destruction by the waves which destroyed and re-built it several times before now?

6 Describe the previous positions of Spurn Head. How often does it seem to change position?

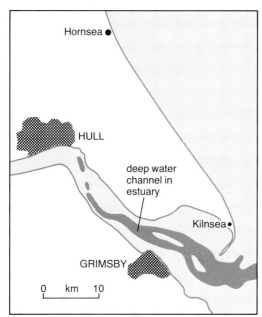

Figure 3.57(a) The location of Spurn Head in North Humberside.

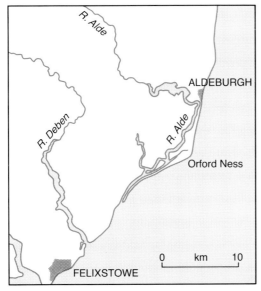

Figure 3.58 Orford Ness, a spit on the Suffolk coast.

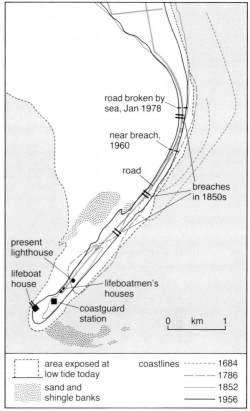

Figure 3.57(b) Details of recent positions of Spurn Head, and some of the human uses of the spit.

Figure 3.59 Spurn Head from the air.

If Spurn is allowed to be destroyed, then the lifeboat station and the lifeboat men's houses would be lost, along with the pilot's jetty and the coastguard look-out. It would take the lifeboat an extra half an hour to get out into the North Sea from Grimsby, the nearest alternative place. There would no longer be as much shelter in the estuary, and the shipping channels in the estuary would probably shift.

But can Spurn be kept forever? If so how, and who pays? Certainly not the Yorkshire Naturalist Trust who own it, because they cannot afford to spend a lot on defences. One answer might be to stop wasting money on sea defences and in-stead to plant salt marsh and lyme and marram grasses on the *inside* of the spit to let sand accumulate there. Then the whole spit would gradually be allowed to move westwards as new land is created on the estuary side.

We can see from the study of Spurn Head that each time the new spit forms it lines up with a new position of the East Yorkshire coast. This illustrates clearly how much coastal erosion has happened there.

7 Look at Figure 3.60 which shows the amount by which the cliff has receded, (moved back), between 1852 and 1952. Trace the present-day outline, and draw in the coastline of 1852 by using a scale of 1 mm to 50 m (this is rather exaggerated, but it would be impossible for you to draw it with a smaller scale).

8 In which section of the coast was there most erosion over these 100 years?

9 What has the average rate of erosion per year been at Easington?

10 Where has the material eroded from this coast probably been taken to?

11 Pick out from the figures and the text half a dozen reasons why the loss of Spurn Head would be a bad thing.

12 Who should pay for its preservation? Should it even be preserved, or should we let nature takes its course?

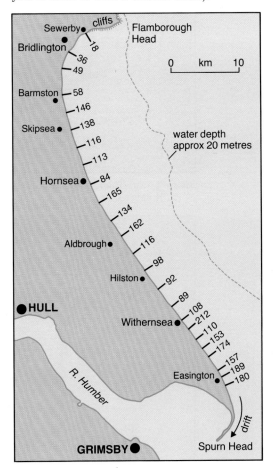

Figure 3.60 Amount of erosion along the Yorkshire coast between 1852 and 1952. Loss of land has been measured in metres.

Figure 3.61 Erosion in cliffs in dune sand at Hemsby, Norfolk.

How can this rapid erosion be prevented? Should we try to prevent it? There are several possible solutions to the first question.

Preventing Coastal Erosion

a) *Groynes* are one possible solution. Groynes have been built along this section of coast to trap sand and stop it from being taken down to Spurn. Of course this could have a bad effect on Spurn Head. Can you think why? By keeping the beach in place, there is a buffer zone between the sea and the cliff. The beach protects the cliff from the force of the waves. The energy of the waves is spent on moving beach material instead of on attacking the cliff.

b) *Sea walls* can be built of concrete, like artificial cliff walls. The problem with them is that they are solid, and simply stop the waves. The wave's energy gradually attacks and undermines the sea wall.

c) *Tetrapods* are similar to revêtments. They are three-legged lumps of concrete dumped at the coast. When the waves break on them the water can move through them but will lose its energy quickly and the cliff will be protected.

d) *Revêtments* may be used. Boulders are dumped at the coast and enclosed in strong wire mesh or netting. This also forms a barrier, but it is not completely solid, and lets the waves lose their energy more gradually.

Figure 3.62 Four types of coastal defences.
(a) Groynes at Overstrand, Norfolk.

(b) Sea walls at Hornsea, Humberside.

(c) Tetrapods at Muscat harbour, Oman.

(d) Revêtments at Overstrand, Norfolk.

Exercise

1 Rank these four sea defences in order, from the one that is least ugly to look at to the one that most spoils the appearance of the coast.

2 Which method would probably be the cheapest to install?

3 Which method do you think would be most effective? Why?

4 How would you decide which method of sea defence you would use at a particular site? First think about what you would need to know about the site before you could decide on the best alternative.

Coastal erosion and human interference – positive feedback

Sometimes our attempts to control erosion make the problems worse. Figure 3.63 shows a possible *feedback loop*. In this simple system there is a positive feedback. The initial change (cliff erosion) is increased by the sequence of events. The erosion might have been transferred to a different cliff, but nevertheless the problem still exists.

What are the human consequences of coastal erosion? A number of villages along the East Yorkshire coast have already disappeared into the sea since Roman times.

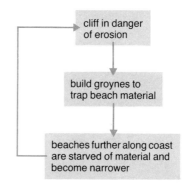

Figure 3.63 A positive feedback loop, showing the knock-on effects of preventing cliff erosion at one point on the coast.

Coastal erosion in Holderness

An article appeared in the *Guardian* newspaper on 23 June 1988 describing the battle to save the latest victim of coastal erosion in Holderness – Mappleton. Two hundred years ago the village was 4 km from the sea. Today an abandoned wooden house, 'The Cabin', has a few metres to go, and the next house is 7 m from the cliff edge. The average rate of erosion now is 1.8 m a year, so Mappleton looks set to join the 29 other villages which have disappeared from the Holderness coast in the last 1000 years. The residents are understandably upset, and one of them has set up a 'Save Mappleton' campaign. Read the newspaper extract on the next page to see what she said about the problem.

One possible way of stopping this erosion is being investigated. It would involve bringing thousands of tonnes of colliery waste from inland and dumping them in the sea off-shore. These banks would use up some of the energy of the sea, and could encourage more beach material to accumulate (gather) there. Research into the plan will cost £1 million, and to put it into operation would probably cost £200 million. Part of the cost might be met by British Coal who already have to spend money on getting rid of coal waste. The rest *might* come from the EEC. The question is, is it worth this cost to fight nature and protect over 300 km² of agricultural land, home to 50 000 people? You would probably think so if you lived there! There might also be more urgency in the plan if there were some major industries on the coast about to lose their plant!

Exercise

1 Which other villages in Holderness appear to be under threat from erosion?

2 Why is it important to find out about the effects of dumping coal waste off-shore before actually beginning the work? (Look back to page 10 if you need some ideas.)

3 Work with a partner. One of you takes the role of a Mappleton resident, the other an official of Humberside County Council. Imagine you have a meeting together. Think about what you would say, then act out the meeting. At the end, discuss whether you have a better understanding of the other person's point of view.

The Save Mappleton campaign is led by Mrs Dorothy Meggitt, whose terraced cottage is half way along Cliff Lane, giving it 50 years at the current erosion rate. She says: "The high tides in the autumn are worst. Combined with a north-easterly wind, they can take huge chunks off. The average erosion is six feet a year but I once saw a 12-foot piece disappear overnight. It's hard for the farmers who are losing land — I have seen a whole field go in my 33 years here.

There are about a dozen houses and farms between the road and the cliff edge and none of us can insure our homes or ask good prices if we want to sell them."

Holderness borough council has offered to rehouse villagers whose homes are in danger, but most people have chosen to stay, says Mrs Meggitt.

Mrs Meggitt's neighbours, Geoffrey and Karen Porter, have bought and moved into a caravan because the house they have owned for

15 years, Ponderosa, is due to be demolished. Mr Porter says: "There used to be two houses, a piece of grass, and a footpath between us and the sea. Now the bedroom is 25 feet from the edge and our sewage tank fell into the sea a few weeks ago. We have lost eight feet of land since the beginning of this year, and depending on the weather, our house has anything between two weeks and two years before it goes."

Figure 3.64 Villagers in Mappleton fight to save their houses. *The Guardian* 23.6.88 © Alexandra Duval Smith

Figure 3.65 A public bath offering a very exposed washing facility on the cliff top at Mappleton.

Coastal dunes

Not all sea coasts have cliffs. Some coasts are backed by *sand dunes*. Dune coasts are particularly vulnerable to erosion, but on the other hand dunes are also a very important natural defence.

About 400 km of the coastline of England and Wales have sand dunes. For almost 100 km the sand dunes are the sole or major sea defence. Not only are sand dunes cheaper and more attractive than sea walls, but they also have other advantages (see Figure 3.66).

Sand dune	Sea wall
1. Offer a broad barrier to flooding and have a reservoir of sand to replace beach loss and thus reduce wave power.	Offer a narrow barrier to flooding and no reservoir of material so waves keep their power.
2. Dunes absorb wave energy.	Sea walls do not absorb wave energy.
3. Dunes do not allow water levels to build up. If a breach occurs flooding is usually gradual and shallow.	Sea walls allow water levels to build up. If a breach occurs flooding is likely to be sudden and deep.
4. Successive dune ridges provide a series of coast defences.	Sea walls usually offer just a single defence.
5. Vegetated dunes have powers to regenerate and increase their height.	Sea walls cannot regenerate or build themselves.

Source: Ranwell & Boar, 1986.

Figure 3.66 A comparison of sand dunes with sea walls from the point of view of coastal protection.

Exercise

1 What *additional* advantages are there in protecting a coast with dunes rather than a concrete wall? Think about vegetation, wildlife, recreation, and scenery.

2 List some of the types of recreational uses of sand dune coasts.

Dunes are under threat from over-use, and need some protection. The Nature Conservancy Council is one organisation which is working to protect threatened sections of Britain's dune coast. One of their success stories is at Camber in Sussex.

Dune restoration: Camber, Sussex

The Problem

1930s   Cars were driven all over the dunes as people tried to get as close to the beach as possible. In one day in 1936, 4600 vehicles were counted.

1940s   The dunes were used for military training for amphibious vehicles (able to travel on land and water). By 1945 most of the dune vegetation had been destroyed.

1960s   The whole centre section of the dunes was practically bare. Sand was starting to invade roads and buildings inland, as there was no vegetation to hold it in place.

1967   Restoration of the dunes began.

Figure 3.67 A signboard explaining dune restoration work at Camber.

The Solution

Figure 3.67 illustrates the types of restoration work which were done at Camber. By 1980 the dunes had been raised to a height of 6 m, and the shoreline advanced 5–10 m seaward. The cost of the restoration was £100 000, and much of the success of this scheme lay in informing the public about what was being done, and why.

Figure 3.68 Dune look-out with controlled access car park, Parnassia.

Heritage Coasts

Looking back over this unit on coasts, what do you see as the main threats to Britain's coasts? Can you classify them into those which are entirely natural and those which result from human interference?

To protect the stretches of coastline that are still unspoilt, the Countryside Commission created the idea of a Heritage Coast. Already 43 such stretches of coast have been identified. Many of these sections of coast have a Heritage Coast Officer, whose main job is to identify problems and their causes, encourage co-operation in resolving conflicts, and to arrange for small-scale practical work, such as mending fences and replacing stiles, to be done. This is done to preserve the natural coastal features, and to protect the stretches of coastline that are still unspoilt.

Changes in sea level

In the last Ice Age, Britain was covered with ice roughly as far south as a line joining the Thames and the Severn. The ice was thickest and heaviest in the north, especially in Scotland. This great weight of ice made Britain sink very slightly into the underlying rocks. What would have happened when the ice finally melted, about 10 000 years ago?

First, the melting ice would have run into the sea and raised the world sea level. Secondly, the land would have recovered very slowly from the great weight of the ice which had been on it, and would have risen very gradually. The first change is easy to understand, you can imagine the second one. Think about carrying a very heavy load on your shoulders. When the load is removed you feel lighter, as though your shoulders are floating upwards. Figure 3.69 illustrates both changes.

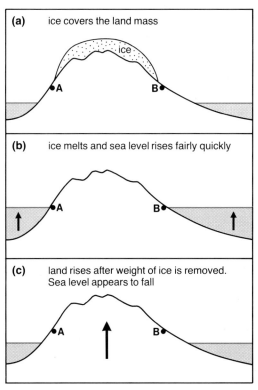

Figure 3.69 A cross section across the northern part of Britain during and after the last Ice Age.

Exercise

1 Which part of Britain would rise up most – north or south? Explain your answer.

2 Copy the sketch of a river mouth in ice age Britain (Figure 3.70) Imagine that the sea level rises 10 m at the end of the ice age, and shade in the new coastline. The feature you have just drawn is called a *ria*. It is a flooded river valley.

4 A ria makes an excellent harbour – explain why.

5 A ria can be an inconvenience to transport networks. Can you suggest why? What could be done to make transport easier near a ria?

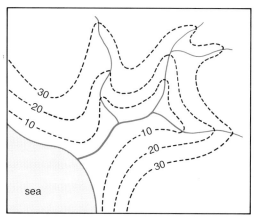

Figure 3.70 A river valley close to the coast in Ice Age Britain.

The Rance estuary is a good example of a ria. It also has one of the world's largest *tidal ranges* – that is the difference between high tide and low tide level. As early as the twelfth century local people were building small reservoirs in part of the Rance valley. These filled up when the tide came in, then as the tide went out, the water drove mill wheels. Today this tidal ebb and flow is used to drive turbines to produce electricity in a power station built at a dam across the Rance estuary (Figure 3.71).

Figure 3.71 The Rance Valley power station, France.

Figure 3.72 A raised beach at Bennan Head, Arran.

This power station can produce 550 mkw (million kilowatts) of electricity each year. Lock gates have been built to allow boats to bypass the dam.

A ria is formed where there is a net (over-all) rise in sea level. If there is a net fall in sea level at the end of the ice age, another type of feature may be formed – a *raised beach*.

6 In which part of Britain would you expect to find raised beaches? Give a reason for your answer.

7 Draw a sketch from the photo in Figure 3.72 and label it clearly to show the old beach and cliff, the present day beach and cliff, slope angles and the appearance of the surfaces.

The Effects of Glaciation

In the past two million years Britain has experienced several *glaciations*, when much of the land was covered in ice sheets and glaciers. The last ice sheet melted about 10 000 years ago, and we have probably left the ice age behind. Of course, we might just be in one of the *interglacials*, (warm periods), between two glaciations ...!

During these glaciations, the average annual temperature in Britain fell by −6°C to −9°C. When it snowed, the snow collected and gradually compressed (compacted) the layers underneath to form ice. This can take many years. These *ice masses* developed in hollows on mountain sides, and gradually became so large that they started to move down the old river valleys as *glaciers*. It still remained cold, the glaciers grew larger, and eventually they joined together until most of Britain was covered in a huge *ice sheet*. Britain would have looked then a bit like Greenland does today.

The ice has had an enormous effect on our scenery. A glacier can erode a huge amount, and very quickly, as it moves down a valley, especially because it nearly fills the valley up completely!

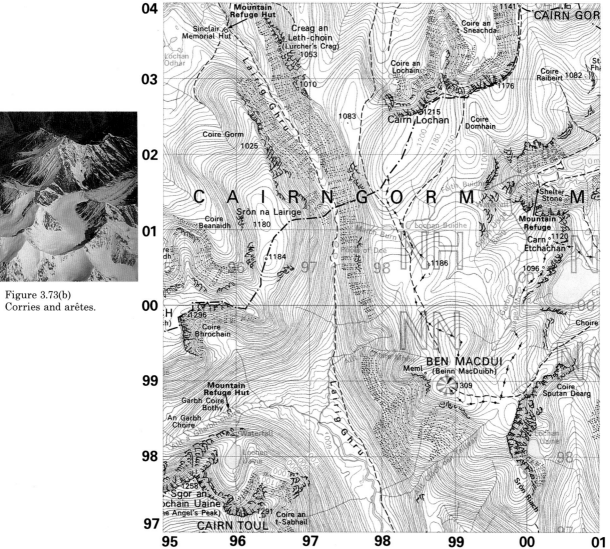

Figure 3.73(b)
Corries and arêtes.

Figure 3.73(a) An extract from a 1:50 000 Ordnance Survey map of part of the Cairngorms of Scotland, showing some glacially eroded features.

The deeper the glacier, the more erosion it achieves. Small glaciers in side valleys cannot erode as deeply as the main valley glacier. When the ice has melted these smaller side valleys are left hanging above the main valley.

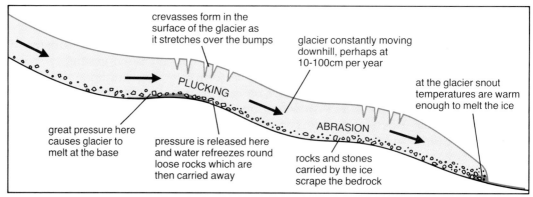

Figure 3.74(a) Some of the processes of glacial erosion.

(b) Snow accumulating into ice in the Swiss Alps.

(c) The Mer de Glace.

Figure 3.75(a) Miller's Dale, a river eroded valley in Derbyshire.

These processes do not just happen at the base of the glacier on the valley bottom, but also along its sides. If we look at a valley cross-section we can see the effect.

The glacier begins in a *corrie*, a hollow up on the mountain side (Figure 3.76). Corries are also called cwms in Wales and cirques in France. We have some fine examples in Britain – you can see several in the map extract in Figure 3.73.

Figure 3.75(b) Flam Valley, a glacially eroded valley in Norway.

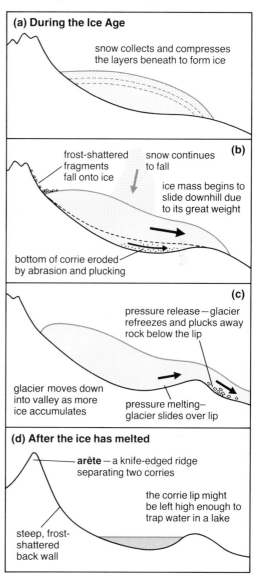

Figure 3.76 Stages in the formation of a corrie.

Exercise

1 Figure 3.74(a) shows the glacier eroding by *abrasion* and by *plucking*. Use the diagram to explain the differences between these processes.

2 Compare the two valleys in Figure 3.75. How many differences can you list? Look at the slopes, the width and depth of the valley, the valley floor, and the tributary valleys.

Map Exercises

1 Using Figure 3.73 match the grid reference with the feature:

956000	corrie without lake
960980	ribbon lake
956996	arête
978975	hanging valley
010020	corrie with lake
995023	glaciated U-shaped valley

2 There are about 18 corries shown in this extract. Look at each one and identify the direction it faces. For example, the corrie at 946988 is facing south east.

What do you notice about the direction most corries face? Can you explain your answer?

3 Using Figure 3.73(a) on page 83 sketch the cross-section of the Lairig Ghru Valley from 965974 to 989989. Describe the shape of the valley you have drawn.

4 Write a description of the area for tourists who might wish to walk in the area. Mention the type of scenery they will see, the paths available, the distances they might have to walk, and what to do if they get into difficulties. What other advice should tourists be given?

Tourism in the Cairngorms, Scotland

The map extract in Figure 3.73(a) is of part of the Cairngorm mountains. Just to the north of the area shown is the Cairngorm skiing area. The mountain slopes, which are usually snow-covered in winter, are ideal for skiing. The sketch map (Figure 3.77) of the ski slopes and surrounding areas shows some of the developments that are associated with the skiing industry.

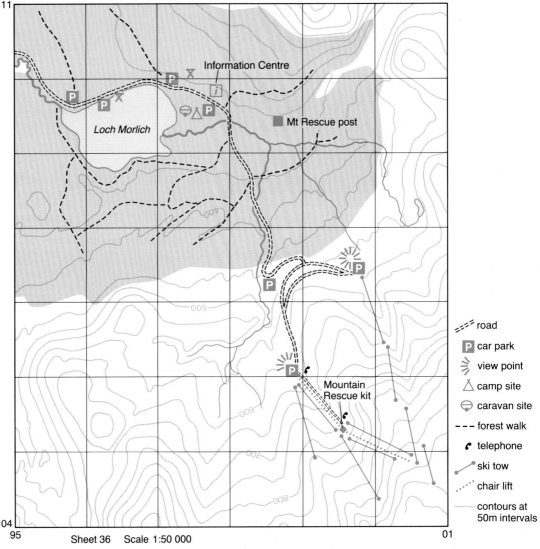

Figure 3.77 Some of the developments associated with the skiing industry in the Cairngorms.

Sheet 36   Scale 1:50 000

Figure 3.78 The Fort William area of north west Scotland, and the site of the proposed ski development on the northern slopes of Aonach Mor.

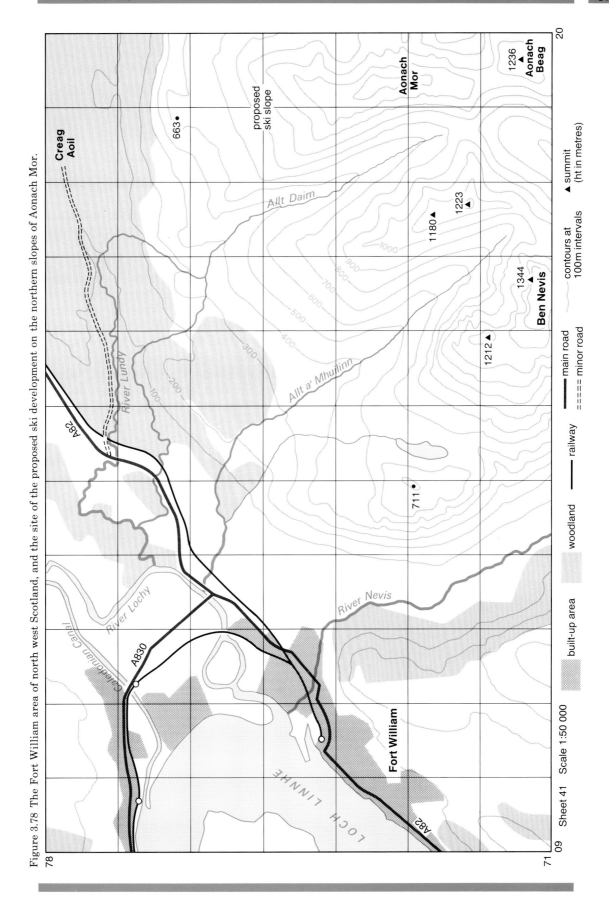

Exercise

1 List all the facilities that have been provided in the local area:
   a) particularly for skiers; and
   b) for any tourist visitors.

2 What sort of benefits would the skiing holiday industry bring to the local area?

As well as the benefits you have listed, there will be some costs.

- The ski-tows and chairlifts are permanent features and may spoil the natural scenery.
- Car parks are ugly, both when empty stretches of concrete, *and* when full of cars.
- More litter is dropped by all the visitors.
- There is heavier traffic on local roads, which weren't built for it.
- Tourists have to be accommodated in hotels, guest houses, camp sites etc. which might be built in prominent positions and might not fit in with the local area.
- The fragile moorland vegetation gets badly trampled, especially when the snow cover is thin, and if the vegetation is killed the soil can be eroded easily.
- Snow is what the skiers want, yet when it snows heavily and skiers try to reach the ski slopes, they are sometimes trapped in their cars. Farmers and other local people sometimes resent the time and money spent on rescuing these people, and on keeping the roads to the ski slopes open, rather than the local routes.

Now that you have thought about both the benefits and the costs of developing a ski resort, assess this plan to open a ski slope on the slope of Aonach Mor near Fort William. Figure 3.78 shows the location of the area under consideration.

Exercise

1 Why do you think this site was chosen for a possible ski slope?

2 Make a simple copy of the sketch and on your copy mark the developments you think will be necessary to open the site up for skiing.

3 Work in groups of five. Each of you will take the role of one of the following people who might have an opinion about this development. First, on your own work out your thoughts about the scheme and then put them to the rest of your group in turn. You will need to re-read all the material on the Cairngorm ski slopes first. When you have discussed the proposal in your groups, write a summary of the good and bad effects it might have, and what your final opinion is.

Hotelier in Fort William – at the moment most of your trade is in the summer, and it's hardly worth opening in the winter.

Nature Conservancy Council – you are concerned about the threat to the environment to both plant and animal life. (Read page 152 to give you an idea of the problems.)

Local Councillor in Fort William – tourism is already quite an important source of income in Fort William, and many facilities for tourists already exist. Fort William can be reached fairly easily by both road and rail.

Farmer at Creag Aoil – you live close to the access road to the ski slopes. You rear sheep and deer (for venison). You have lived all your life in this remote and tranquil spot.

Doctor in Glasgow – you are a keen skier and often travel to the Cairngorm slopes at weekends. Aonach Mor would be nearer for you so you could spend longer on the slopes!

To see a glacier today you would have to travel to an area which is further north or at a higher altitude than Britain. The nearest glaciers to us are in Norway or Switzerland. Glaciers in accessible places like these are very popular tourist attractions. In some places guided walks on top of the glacier, and perhaps even inside it in the natural tunnels of the glacier, are available. Others go just to *see* the spectacle of a glacier – which is much bluer than most people imagine.

As a resource, glaciers are mainly important for their scenic beauty. In areas that have been glaciated in the past, tongues of ice have sometimes cut relatively low passes through mountains. These passes can be used today for roads or even railways.

Glacier hazards

Something as remote and slow moving as a glacier can hardly be thought of as a hazard – yet there are some examples. The Hubbard Glacier, a 'galloping glacier' in Alaska, (Figure 3.79(a)) made the news headlines in 1986 when it surged forward at a speed of about 10 m per *day* and blocked the entrance to a fjord (*New Scientist* 2 October 1986). The Hubbard Glacier's last spring to the coast had taken place in the twelfth century. In September 1986 it had moved so far down its valley that it blocked the entrance to Russell Fjord, creating Russell Lake. The level of the lake rose 16.8 m between March and August. Apart from the danger of flooding when the water spilled out of this lake, the local wildlife was threatened. Russell Fjord, a salt water environment, was home to fish, seal and porpoise, among others. These creatures were unable to survive long periods in the fresh water being created.

Glaciers basically pose three different types of threat, illustrated in Figure 3.79(b). Examples of each type can be found in historical records, and in evidence from moraines which mark the old positions of the glacier *snout* (end). In one case the evidence came to light 200 years after the event, when the remains of a chalet was ejected from the snout of the Gauli Glacier in Switzerland. Most examples of the first type date from the seventeenth and eighteenth centuries in Europe, when the climate became colder and harsher, during the Little Ice Age. When building villages and farms, glaciers may have been 2–3 km away, and seemed to pose no immediate threat.

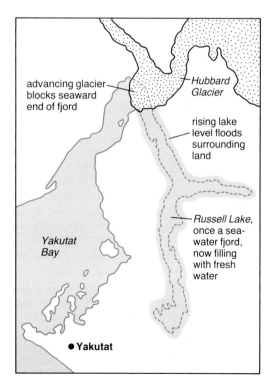

Figure 3.79(a) The creation of a freshwater lake by the advance of the Hubbard Glacier in Alaska.

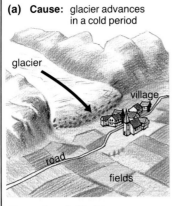

(a) Cause: glacier advances in a cold period

Examples of effects:

1. 1600 — glaciers destroyed 21 houses in Chamonix valley

2. 1820 — Mer de Glace only 20m from village of Les Bois

3. 1743 — Nigardsbreen, Norway, destroyed a farm

4. 1698 — Breidarmörk, farm in Iceland deserted by inhabitants. Ruins disappeared 1712

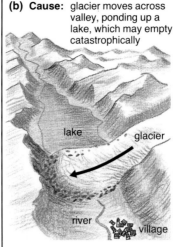

(b) Cause: glacier moves across valley, ponding up a lake, which may empty catastrophically

Examples of effects:

1. 1725 — 1500-2000 people died in village of Ancash in Cordillera Blanca, Peru

2. 1941 — over 6000 people killed and city of Huaraz destroyed in same area

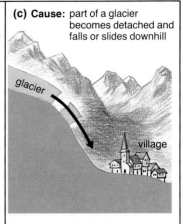

(c) Cause: part of a glacier becomes detached and falls or slides downhill

Examples of effects:

1. 1949 — 6 walkers killed by ice avalanche from Le Tour glacier

2. 1636 — 36 killed and village of Randa damaged by Bies glacier

3. 1736 — 140 buildings in Randa damaged. Proposal to re-site village rejected

Figure 3.79(b) Three types of hazard caused by glaciers.

Exercise

1 Study Figure 3.79(b).
  a) Which type of hazard would there be most warning about?
  b) Which type of hazard is most likely to cause a disaster?
  c) Suggest how the disastrous effect of any of these hazards could be prevented or reduced.

Avalanches

Avalanches are another hazard in a snow covered mountain area. The great weight of snow on a mountainside sometimes causes a mass of snow to slide down very rapidly. This avalanching can be set off by skiers crossing a slope, or by unusually warm temperatures. Heavy snow can also trigger an avalanche by adding further weight to an already unstable slope. Various types of protection against avalanching can be seen in areas likely to suffer avalanches, such as the

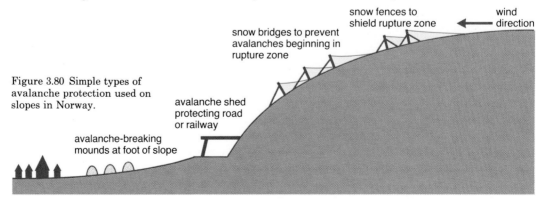

Figure 3.80 Simple types of avalanche protection used on slopes in Norway.

Norwegian mountains. In west and north Norway steep slopes, a low timber line, high precipitation (rain and snowfall) and fluctuations (changes) of temperature in winter all combine to make avalanches likely.

The types of protection used in Norway against avalanching are shown in Figure 3.80. The newspaper article in Figure 3.81 illustrates the damage which avalanches can do in inhabited areas. This is yet another example of how the human use of the environment can increase a hazard. When no one lived in the high mountains, avalanches were a natural occurrence, not a hazard. Now that we have built villages, ski resorts and roads to make use of the environment, an avalanche is a life-threatening hazard.

Exercise

1 The timber line is the level above which trees are unable to grow. Why would a low timber line make the avalanche risk greater?

2 Look back to the section on mass wasting on page 36. What similarities are there between the causes of avalanches and the causes of landslides?

3 How can the risk to human life from avalanches be reduced in mountain areas?

4 Read the newspaper article entitled 'Blizzard chaos in Austrian resorts'.
a) Where did the avalanche happen?
b) What damage did it do in Saint Anton?
c) What two causes are suggested for triggering the avalanche?
d) What other difficulties did the heavy snow cause?

Blizzard chaos in Austria

A massive avalanche roared down a mountainside and hit a skiing village in western Austria yesterday morning, killing seven people and injuring at least 30.

The tragedy brought to 10 the number killed in Austrian avalanches at the weekend. On Saturday a Swede was killed in another avalanche at St Anton while two more people, one a West German skier on a chairlift, died in similar incidents at Biberwier and Berwang the same day.

Yesterday's avalanche, the like of which has not been seen by local people in more than 80 years, hit the village of St Anton, which is favoured by continental and British holidaymakers on skiing package tours. More than 400 rescuers, including villagers, ski in-

structors and fire department officials, as well as "avalanche dogs" and several helicopters, combed the mountain for survivors.

Those who died were either suffocated or crushed in the rubble of buildings hit by the avalanche, police in the Tyrol said. Herr Gerd Schmidt, a West German holidaymaker, said: "It was like a train running down the hill."

The avalanche struck at around 6.50am, destroying a number of houses in the valley and burying holiday homes and their inhabitants in up to 40 ft of packed snow.

Most were dug out alive but some, still asleep at the early hour, "were gone before they knew what has hit them", according to one regional police official. "The older

generation I talked to said it was the worst they had seen in 80 years."

Between 30,000 and 45,000 people due to go home from their skiing holidays were still stranded late yesterday at Alpine resorts in western Austria. Around St Anton, Lech and Zurs in Vorarlberg province, more than 30 inches of new snow were reported to have fallen in the previous 24 hours. The combination of such heavy falls and mild temperatures were cited by officials as the likely causes of the avalanche.

The blizzard also made Vorarlberg impassable, as railway lines and roads were buried under feet of drifting snow. The main line between Innsbruck, the Tyrolean capital, and Zurich in Switzerland also remained closed.

Figure 3.81 *The Times* 14.3.88

Desposition by glaciers and ice sheets

Rivers erode rock and drop it elsewhere, on a flood plain or a delta for example. The sea erodes cliffs and uses the material to build beaches. In the same way, glaciers also carry the eroded rock with them, and drop it when they can no longer carry it. Remember that the key to this is *energy*. When the glacier has no more energy, because it is not moving and the ice is very thin, all the material carried in it is deposited. This usually happens at the glacier's snout.

If the glacier's snout is at one place for a long time, a heap of material will build up. This heap is called *terminal moraine* (Figure 3.82). The area in front of the glacier snout is the *outwash plain*. The sand and gravels dropped here by the *meltwater stream* are sometimes excavated for building materials, if they are fairly accessible. *Ground moraine* (or *till*) has also been left under the ice sheets which covered lowland areas of Britain. In some places the moraine has been shaped and squeezed into egg shaped lumps called *drumlins*. These often occur in swarms and form a distinctive landscape (Figure 3.83).

Sometime huge lumps of ice became detached from the ice sheet and were embedded in moraine. As these separate lumps of ice gradually melted, the ground surface above them collapsed, leaving a hole which we now call a *kettle hole*.

Figure 3.82 The formation of deposits of terminal moraine at a glacier snout.

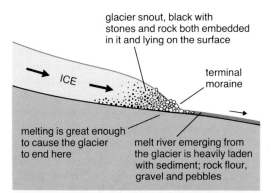

glacier snout, black with stones and rock both embedded in it and lying on the surface

ICE

terminal moraine

melting is great enough to cause the glacier to end here

melt river emerging from the glacier is heavily laden with sediment; rock flour, gravel and pebbles

Figure 3.83 A swarm of drumlins at Ribblehead in the Yorkshire Dales.

CHAPTER FOUR

Weather and Climate

Britain's climate

The maps in Figure 4.1 show certain aspects of the weather in Britain in 1987.
The data come from a journal, *Weather*, produced by the meteorological society.
This journal has a section in it each month giving a variety of weather
measurements for stations all over the country.

   The weather in Britain can be very different from year to year, month to month
and day to day. That is why some people think living here is never dull, and why
the weather is a very popular topic of conversation. The maps in Figure 4.2 show
two unusual aspects of the weather in Britain in 1976.

Figure 4.1 Three aspects of the weather in Britain in June 1987:

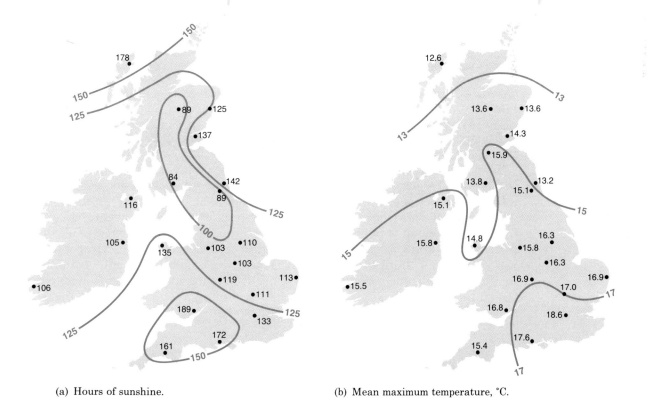

(a) Hours of sunshine.

(b) Mean maximum temperature, °C.

Exercise

Imagine that you were going on holiday in June 1987, and were looking for the best place to spend a holiday lying on the beach, sun-bathing and swimming. Use the three maps in Figure 4.1 to decide where it would be best to go. You will need a piece of tracing paper and three coloured pencils.

1 First lay the tracing paper over the map showing days without rain. Trace the outline of Britain. Decide that you want 11 or more dry days. On your tracing shade blue all the parts of Britain which had fewer than 11 dry days.

2 Now lay the tracing over the map showing the mean (average) maximum temperatures. Imagine that you want this to be more than 17°C. Shade in green everywhere that was too cool.

3 Finally shade in brown all the areas that had fewer than 150 hours of sunshine.

4 Is there any part of Britain left unshaded? There should be. Use an atlas to find the names of some resorts that you might have gone to, if you could have known what the weather was going to be like in advance!

5 Did you expect that the area you have found would be a good area for fine holiday weather? Why?

6 What other aspects of the weather might a holidaymaker like to know about?

7 What was unusual about the weather in 1976?

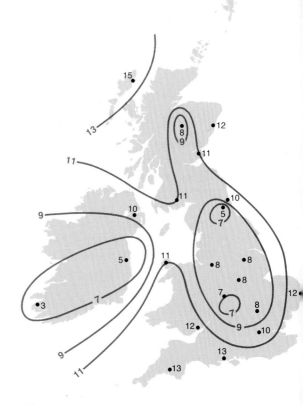

Figure 4.1(c) Number of days without rain.

8 In what parts of Britain was the weather most different from usual?

We shall return to 1976 later in this chapter, as the unusual weather conditions that summer had a big impact on people.

So, what makes up the weather? Many different things, as the newspaper map in Figure 4.3 shows. Maps like this appear on the television each evening, and in lots of daily newspapers.

Although the weather changes from day to day, and year to year, we have a certain *climate* which is fairly fixed. The climate is really the average of all our weather. We know for instance that Britain won't become a desert or a frozen waste next year. Both the daily weather and the long-term climate are influenced by three factors, outlined in Figure 4.4. The driving force behind this machine is the sun, in the same way as it was for the geomorphological machine (page 42).

9 From the map in Figure 4.3, list all the different aspects of the weather which can be measured.

10 What was the weather forecast for the area that you live in on this particular date?

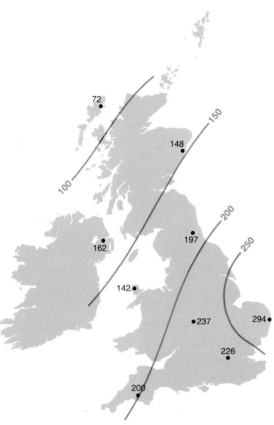

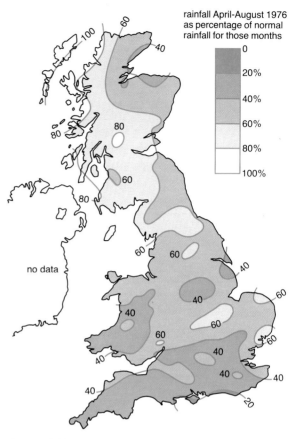

rainfall April-August 1976
as percentage of normal
rainfall for those months

Figure 4.2(a) Extra sunshine hours, June–August 1976. The map shows the number of hours of sunshine *more than* the average for these months.

(b) Rainfall between April and August 1976 as a percentage of the normal rainfall.

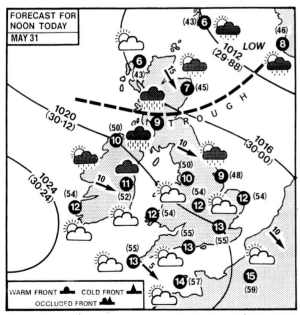

Black circles show temperatures expected in Centigrade (Fahrenheit in brackets). Arrows indicate wind direction and speed in mph. Pressure in millibars (inches in brackets).

Figure 4.3 A weather map from The Daily Telegraph, for 31 May 1989.

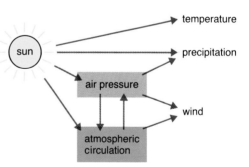

Figure 4.4 Factors which influence climate.

Sunshine and temperatures

The amount and intensity of the sunshine we receive affects the temperature. Table 1 gives figures for the number of hours of sunshine per day in Felixstowe, and the average temperature.

Table 1   Sunshine hours and temperatures in Felixstowe

	Jan	Feb	Mar	Apr	May	Jun	Jul	Aug	Sep	Oct	Nov	Dec
Number of hours/day	1.9	2.7	4.5	5.7	7.2	7.6	7.1	6.6	5.4	3.8	2.2	1.7
Av. temp °C	4	4	6	8	11	15	17	17	15	12	7	5

Exercise

1 Use the figures in Table 1 to draw two line graphs, one showing the number of hours of sunshine per day through the year, and one showing the average temperature. Put the months of the year along the x (horizontal) axis.

2 Describe both graphs as fully as possible. Mention the variation in temperature and in hours of sunshine over the year. Is there much difference from one season to another? When are the sunniest and the least sunny times of the year? What is the range of temperature? Note also the link between the two graphs – what is it?

The amount of sunshine varies through the year because of the tilt of the earth, and the fact that it orbits (goes around) the sun once a year (Figure 4.5). For part of the year the northern hemisphere is tilted away from the sun (i). But as the earth moves round the sun, the sun begins to shine equally on the northern and southern hemispheres (ii). Eventually the northern hemisphere is tilted towards the sun (iii). As the earth completes its orbit, the sun will again concentrate equally on both hemispheres (iv), before the earth gets back to its first position (i).

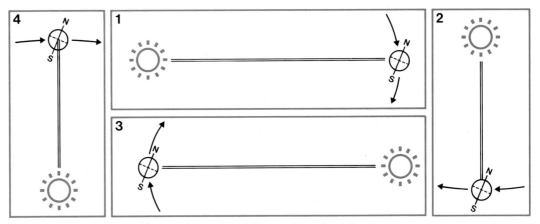

Figure 4.5 The relative positions of the earth and the sun throughout the year.

3 Draw one diagram showing the sun with the four separate positions around it. Label each position of the earth with the months June, September, December and March. (Remember, Britain is in the northern hemisphere, so you can tell when it is June because we have our summer then; look when the sun is concentrating its rays on the northern hemisphere.)

4 Which part of the earth do the sun's rays concentrate on twice in this cycle?

The tilt of the earth changes the angle that the sun's rays hit the earth. You can actually see the difference yourself, if you make observations over a few months.

5 You need to find a tall post (or borrow a friend who's stopped growing). Measure the length of the shadow of the post (or person) at noon (GMT) on the same day every week for a few months. This could be a class project at school. When the shadow is long, the sun is low in the sky – you could even work out the angle with some simple maths (Figure 4.6). If you draw a graph of your results, you will see a steady change in the length of the shadow over the months. The shorter the shadow, the higher the sun is in the sky (and the larger its angle of elevation). The longer the shadow, the lower the sun is in the sky, and the smaller its angle above the horizon.

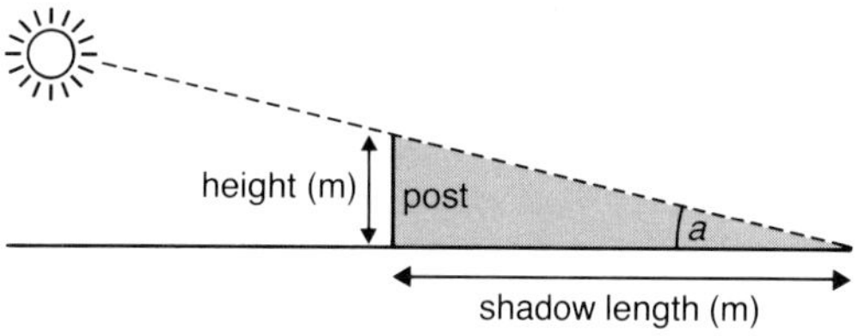

$$\text{tangent } a = \frac{\text{height}}{\text{shadow length}}$$

Figure 4.6 A method to use when calculating the angle of elevation of the sun.

6 When would you expect the shadow to be at its shortest? Why?

When the sun is apparently higher in the sky, its rays are more concentrated on the ground, so the ground gets hotter. Also, when the sun is lower in the sky the distance the rays have to travel through the atmosphere is greater, and more of the *radiation* can be absorbed or lost.

The sun's rays are able to heat land up much faster than water. This is partly because water masses are always moving, and carrying the heated water away from the surface. In fact, it takes five times as long to heat up a mass of water by the same amount as an equal mass of land. But water also cools down very slowly – again because a lot of the heat has been transferred down through the water. We can see the effect that this has on our climate by drawing temperature graphs for two towns, one inland, a long way from the sea, and the other for a town on the same latitude (ie. the same distance from the sun) but at the coast, and therefore strongly affected by the water temperature.

Table 2   Average monthly temperatures for two towns in the British Isles (°C)

	Jan	Feb	Mar	Apr	May	Jun	Jul	Aug	Sep	Oct	Nov	Dec	Temp Range
Town A	4	4	6	9	12	15	17	17	14	10	7	4	?
Town B	7	7	8	9	12	14	15	15	14	12	9	8	?

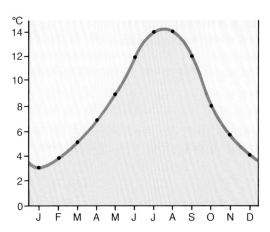

Figure 4.7 Average temperatures at town C, a town in Britain.

Exercise

1 Using the information given in Table 2, draw line graphs of the temperatures at these two towns. Use the same axes to make it easy to compare the temperatures.

2 Which town is warmest in summer, A or B?

3 Which town is warmest in winter, A or B?

4 Work out the *temperature range* at each town. The temperature range is the maximum temperature minus minimum temperature. Does A or B have the greatest range?

5 Is town A or town B closest to the sea? Explain your answer.

6 Now look at the temperature graph for town C in Figure 4.7. Copy and complete the following table, comparing temperatures at the three towns.

	Minimum Temperature	Maximum Temperature	Temperature Range
Town A			
Town B			
Town C			

7 Is town C further north or further south than towns A and B? Give your reasons.

8 Finally, look in an atlas and find Aberdeen, Cambridge and Valentia. These are the three towns A, B and C. Which is which? How do you know?

Altitude and temperature

Another factor which affects the temperature is the height of land, the *altitude*. In general, the temperature falls about 0.6°C for every 100 metres you rise. You experience this if you climb a mountain. For example, if you started from Fort William and climbed Ben Nevis you would rise from sea level to 1344 metres above sea level. This is approximately 13 × 100 metres, so the temperature would fall 0.6°C × 13. If it is 17°C in Fort William, what would the temperature probably be at the top of Ben Nevis?

Dust particles and temperature

One other natural factor seems to have an effect on temperature – that is, major volcanic eruptions. As the sun's rays travel towards the earth, some of the solar radiation is absorbed by tiny particles in the atmosphere. The more particles there are, the less radiation reaches the surface. There is now good evidence that major volcanic eruptions do cause a slight fall in temperature immediately afterwards. Two examples will illustrate this:

A In 1815, Tambora near Java exploded and threw more than 10^{11} tonnes of ash and debris into the air. 1816 was a 'Summerless Year'; in the Eastern USA it snowed in June, and continuous frost in August destroyed most of the harvest.

B Krakatoa ejected more than 50 million tonnes of dust into the atmosphere in 1883. This event produced a worldwide fall in temperature of 0.5°C.

Natural events are not the only ones to put dust particles into the atmosphere. Factories burning coal, open cast mines, and farming land until it becomes desert-like are all ways in which humans can increase the number of particles in the atmosphere.

Exercise

1 Look at Figure 4.8 which compares hours of winter sunshine at Kew (on the outskirts of London) and in Central London. What trend can be seen in both lines?

2 What, approximately, was the lowest winter sunshine level recorded at the London weather centre, and when was this?

3 By how much has winter sunshine increased at the London weather centre? Can you suggest why this has happened?

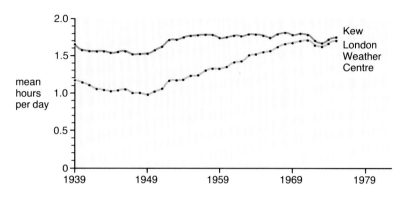

Figure 4.8 A comparison of the number of hours of winter sunshine (between December and February) at the London weather centre and at Kew gardens.

This work on the effects of air pollution will be followed up later on pages 104 and 111 because air pollution also affects fog and rainfall.

Cities and temperature

Humans can influence temperatures in another way – by building cities. This creates 'urban heat islands'. The dark coloured walls, buildings and roads of the city absorb a lot of the sun's radiation during the day, and release it at night. There is also a great deal of artificial heat produced by industrial, commercial and domestic users. All in all, London has been estimated to be about 1.3°C warmer on average than the surrounding countryside.

Exercise

1 Look at Figure 4.9 which shows the *minimum* temperatures in London on one day in 1959.

a) Describe the distribution of temperatures as fully as you can. Mention where it was coldest, where it was warmest, and the amount of difference between these areas.

b) Why do the isotherms bend in towards the centre of London in the east? (look at the built up area, and the River Thames).

c) What effects might these slightly higher temperatures have on plants and animals in the city of London?

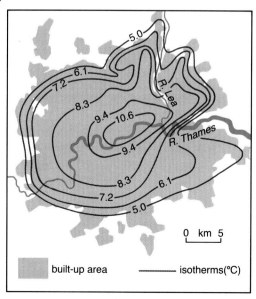

Figure 4.9 Minimum temperatures in London on a day in May 1959.

Temperature Hazards

Extreme temperatures can be hazardous, although looking back to Figure 1.6(b) on page 15 they were only mentioned once as a disaster causing loss of life – in North America. Extremely low temperatures are often associated with snow and blizzards, and it is the latter that cause most problems.

One of the most extreme winters in recent years was experienced in the United States in 1976/77. New records were set for snowfall – 4561 mm in Buffalo, and 7061 mm in Boonville, New York. Not only was the snow phenomenally deep, but the cold was so intense that the snowdrifts froze solid and broke the blades of the snow ploughs. Even Niagara Falls froze! The city of Buffalo was cut off, and had to have troops airlifted in with supplies of food and fuel. Thousands of tonnes of snow were regularly sent by train to be dumped in areas where they could not cause a flood as they melted.

Heatwaves have an added hazard which often occurs at the same time – drought. Heatwaves have been experienced in Southern Europe, most recently in 1988 when temperatures in Greece reached 47°C. 31 people died during that heatwave, mainly from heart trouble brought on by the extreme temperatures. Heat plus drought leads to water shortages and the threat of fire. Forest fires in Greece in the same summer claimed at least another 56 lives.

Atmospheric Circulation

The equator is the part of the earth which receives most sunshine, but it does not go on getting hotter and hotter. This is because of air and water movements, which take the heat away from the equator and transfer it towards the poles, where very little sunshine is received.

Why does this happen? Think about a hot air balloon. When the flame is lit, the air in the balloon heats up and it rises. When all the fuel is used up and the air cools, it sinks back to earth. At the equator, the land gets hot and heats up the air next to it by *conduction*. This air then rises because hot air is less dense (heavy) than cold air. Where air is rising, there is low air pressure. Meanwhile, at the poles the cold air is sinking. Where air is sinking there is high air pressure. A simple circulation will result (Figure 4.10(a)).

Cold air moves from the pole to the equator to replace the rising warm air. High in the atmosphere, air moves towards the poles to complete the circuit. The circulation is not quite this simple though, because the earth itself is spinning round. This breaks up the simple loop into three sections (Figure 4.10(b)).

Looking at this figure, you would expect winds to blow from 30°N southwards to the equator. These would be northerly winds. Similarly from 30°N winds should blow northwards to latitude 60°N. These would be southerly winds. *But*, again things are not this simple because the spin of the earth deflects the winds to the right of their course in the northern hemisphere (Figure 4.10(c)). You can see in this diagram that the northerly winds *expected* between 30°N and the equator are deflected to their right so that they actually blow north-easterly. The southerly winds expected between 30°N and 60°N are deflected so that they actually blow south-westerly. (Note that in the southern hemisphere the deflection of winds because of the earth's rotation is to the left).

At the beginning of the section on atmospheric circulation, it was noted that both air and water are involved in transferring heat away from the equator to-wards the poles. There are currents of water in the oceans which are similar to the currents of air in the atmosphere. Figure 4.11 shows a very simplified world map of ocean currents. Warm currents begin in the equatorial zones and carry warm water out towards the poles. Cold currents move in the opposite direction.

How does all of this affect us? The maps and diagrams in Figures 4.10 and 4.11

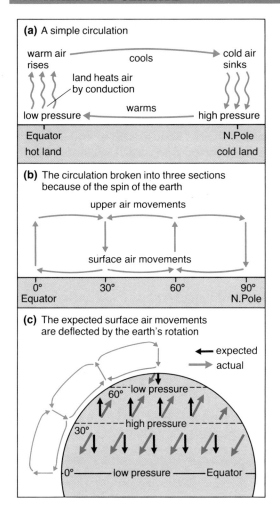

(a) A simple circulation

warm air rises — cools → cold air sinks

land heats air by conduction

low pressure ← warms ← high pressure

Equator / hot land   N.Pole / cold land

(b) The circulation broken into three sections because of the spin of the earth

upper air movements

surface air movements

0°   30°   60°   90°
Equator   N.Pole

(c) The expected surface air movements are deflected by the earth's rotation

← expected
← actual

60° — low pressure
high pressure
30°
0° — low pressure — Equator

Figure 4.10 The world's atmospheric circulation:
(a) A simple circulation – our starting point.
(b) The simple circulation broken into three sections because of the spin of the earth. From this diagram we would expect winds to blow from 30° N due south towards the equator.
(c) We now see that the expected air movements at the earth's surface are deflected by the earth's rotation to produce this pattern of winds.

Figure 4.11 The world's ocean currents.

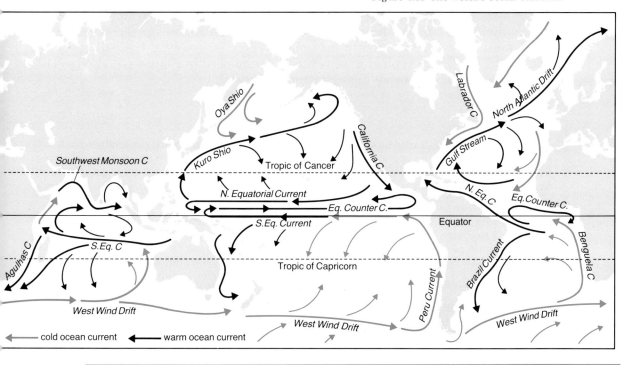

cold ocean current ← warm ocean current

show three important facts about Britain: first, it is in the zone of south westerly winds; second, it is in the low pressure belt where cold air from the north meets warmer air from the south; and third, Britain lies in the path of a warm ocean current, the North Atlantic Drift.

a) *The south westerly wind belt*
The wind in Britain does not *always* blow from the south west, but the main flow of air is from west to east. The south westerly wind is the prevailing one. (For evidence of this, look at page 68 in the section on coastal erosion.) This west–east flow of air affects our temperatures and rainfall.

b) *The low pressure belt of the polar front*
Britain lies under the battle ground where warm air from the south meets cold air from the north. These two different types of air do not mix well, and where they meet, *depressions* form. These are a recipe for rain, as you will see in the next section.

c) *The North Atlantic Drift – a warm ocean current*
Warm water from the tropics is constantly washing around our shores. This warm water brings with it warm air. It is also easier for the sun to evaporate water vapour from warm water, as its temperature does not have to be increased as much. So the warm air over the warm water also contains a lot of water vapour; it is moist. This ocean current therefore affects both Britain's temperatures and rainfall.

Rainfall in Britain

When water vapour condenses in the atmosphere, it condenses around *nuclei*. These nuclei are tiny particles of dust or other matter in the atmosphere. They are essential for condensation to take place. There is, however, basically only one cause of rainfall. The typical water cycle diagram used in Figure 1.4 on page 11 illustrates this basic cause – *rising warm moist air*.

Exercise

1 Arrange the following three statements into a sensible order. Draw a simple diagram to illustrate the cause of rainfall, and add the three statements as labels.

- Air temperature falls higher up. Cool air cannot hold as much moisture as water vapour – so some vapour condenses back into *water droplets*, around condensation nuclei.

- Warm air containing water vapour rises.

- Tiny droplets of water form *clouds*. Droplets collide with one another and grow bigger. The cloud gets darker. Eventually these big drops fall back to earth as rain.

2 What about air that is descending back towards to the earth? Write out the following passage describing what happens when air sinks, and write suitable words or phrases in the spaces.

As air sinks, its temperature will . . . . The warmer air will be able to hold water vapour, so some of the tiny water droplets will . . . . . . into vapour. Clouds will gradually disappear as more of the droplets turn back into an invisible . . . . It is very . . . . . . to rain.

Several different things can happen to force the warm moist air to rise. Whatever the force is, the basic process of rain formation is exactly the same.

a) *High ground can cause air to rise*
Imagine some moist, warm air being gently blown towards Britain. As it reaches the coast it meets hills like the Brecon Beacons, the Cambrian Mountains, Exmoor, the Grampians and so on. The air is forced to rise over these hills. The higher the mountains, the lower the temperature of the air will fall, and the more likely it is to rain. A comparison of a *relief map*, (showing the height and shape of the land), and a map of total rainfall, shows the link between the two very clearly. You can see now why rainfall caused by high ground is called *relief rainfall*.

Exercise

1 Use an atlas to name four areas of Britain which have more than 1000 mm of rain each year.

2 Which parts of Britain have the lowest rainfall each year? Name areas and regions as precisely as you can.

3 Use your atlas to draw a simple cross-section showing the relief across England between Preston and Hull. Label the Pennines, then add the following labels in suitable places:

   Air forced to rise
   Rain falls on hills
   Descending air warms up
   Clouds form over hills
   Condensation as air cools
   Land in the lee of the hills is drier.

b) *Intense heating of the ground can cause air to rise*
Imagine a hot summer's day. The sun has been shining all day, but as late afternoon approaches the clouds gather. People start to complain about the hot, sticky atmosphere. In the early evening there is a thunderstorm and heavy rain. This clears the air and it feels a lot fresher. This type of rainfall often happens in East Anglia where the land is flat — so the cause cannot be high ground. In fact, it is the great heating of the ground which causes the rain. The land gets hotter during the day as the sun beats down on it. The hot land heats up the air next to it. This warm air starts to rise (remember the hot air balloon). More air is drawn in, is heated and rises. We already know what happens to the temperature of the rising air. The processes described on page 102 will take place.

Thunderstorms happen when there are very strong upward currents of air. This may be because of intense heating of the ground. Tiny ice crystals grow in the freezing layers of the cloud and these are swept upwards by the updraft, growing as they go. Thunder clouds become very high and very dark. The upheld ice crystals hold a positive electrical charge which gradually builds up. Eventually it is so great that the charge is discharged down through the clouds to the earth. This is *lightning*. As the lightning passes through the cloud, it instantaneously heats its path up to 15 000°C, and the air expands explosively. This is the *thunderclap*.

In both of these cases, the warm ground heated the air so that the warm air rises in convection currents. It is therefore called *convectional rainfall*.

Exercise

1 Find these towns in your atlas, and then look at Table 3.

Table 3 Monthly rainfall at Norwich and Ilfracombe (mm)

	Jan	Feb	Mar	Apr	May	Jun	Jul	Aug	Sep	Oct	Nov	Dec	Total
Norwich	61	46	38	48	43	43	66	53	58	64	69	61	505
Ilfracombe	104	71	61	58	58	48	76	81	84	112	109	112	974

(a) Which is the wettest month in
   a) Norwich b) Ilfracombe?
(b) Work out the percentage of the total rainfall in each place which falls in the combined months of June, July and August.

2 Explain why Norwich receives quite a large proportion of its rainfall in summer, whereas Ilfracombe does not. You may need to look back to the section on temperature on page 96.

c) *When warm air meets cold air, the warm air rises*
If warm air is moving towards Britain from the south, and cold air is arriving from the north, when they meet something has to give! The warm air which is lighter (remember the hot air balloon) will rise up over the cold air.

The boundary between the two masses is called a *front*. Its position is marked by the formation of cloud along it, as the warm air is chilled. This sort of rainfall occurs very often all over Britain and is called *depressional* or *cyclonic rainfall*. These names come from the type of weather system producing the rainfall – a depression or low pressure system. These are explained in more detail on page 113.

So far, we have seen that for rain to fall, three things must happen:
- The air must contain water vapour.
- There need to be condensation nuclei.
- The air temperature must fall, usually through the air rising.

Cities and rainfall
Humans can accidentally and deliberately affect the amount of rain which falls, in several ways. Look at Table 4 which shows the percentage differences in rainfall and thunderstorms between each city and its surrounding countryside. Figure 4.12 shows some of the possible effects of a city on the atmosphere.

Table 4 The effect of some American cities on rainfall and thunderstorms

City	Percentage increase in rainfall and thunderstorms compared with the area surrounding the city.		Population
	Rainfall	Thunderstorms	
St. Louis	+ 15%	+ 25%	2 400 000
Chicago	+ 17%	+ 38%	8 000 000
Cleveland	+ 27%	+ 42%	2 800 000
Indianapolis	0	0	1 200 000
Washington DC	+ 9%	+ 36%	3 400 000
Houston	+ 9%	+ 10%	3 600 000
New Orleans	+ 10%	+ 27%	1 300 000
Tulsa	0	0	700 000

Exercise

1 Describe the differences in rainfall between these eight city areas and the countryside around them. For which cities is there no effect on rainfall?

2 Explain why thunderstorms are so much more likely over cities (use Figure 4.12 and page 99).

3 Is there any link between the size of a city and its effect on rainfall amounts?

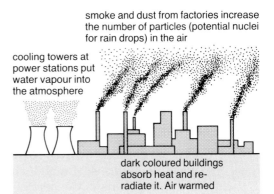

Figure 4.12 Some of the effects a city may have upon the atmosphere around it.

In this example, the effect of the city on rainfall was 'accidental'. In some cases people deliberately try to increase rainfall. This is done by injecting silver iodide crystals into cloud from aeroplanes. These crystals encourage ice crystal growth in the cloud and can cause an increase in rainfall. The method will only work in air which holds water vapour – it would be of no use in a desert. There is also no certainty about where the rain will fall! Cloud seeding is usually used for agricultural reasons, but in the Vietnam War however, the Americans used the method to increase rainfall along a trail used by the Vietcong for bringing in supplies.

Britain's climate – a summary

It is now possible to summarise the climate of different parts of Britain.

Table 5

(i)	Warm to hot summers, cold winters, large temperature range. Low rainfall, slight summer maximum.
(ii)	Cool/warm summers, cold winters. Fairly low rainfall.
(iii)	Cool/warm summers, cool/mild winters. High rainfall.
(iv)	Warm summers, mild winters, very low temperature range. Fairly high rainfall.

Exercise

1 Look at Figure 4.13. Make a simple copy of it onto an outline map of Britain.

2 Match the four areas A, B, C, D, to the four descriptions written out in Table 5. Look back at the sections on temperature and rainfall. When you have matched the descriptions to the areas write them out fully on the correct quadrant of your copy of the map.

3 Which has the greatest contrast from west to east in Britain – rainfall or temperature?

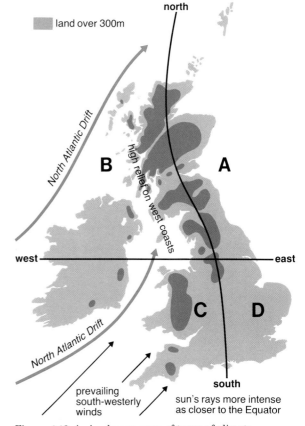

Figure 4.13 A simple summary of types of climate in Britain.

Britain's weather

The last 13 pages have described the *climate* of Britain, ie. the temperature, rainfall, and pressure conditions which we usually expect in different places and at different times of the year. What we actually get each day is the weather, as we saw at the beginning of this chapter. The weather in Britain is mainly affected by the pressure conditions.

Air pressure conditions

Look at Figure 4.14 which shows the air pressures recorded in Europe on a particular day. This is the sort of information a weather forecaster would use to draw *isobars*. An isobar is a line drawn joining places which have the same atmospheric pressure.

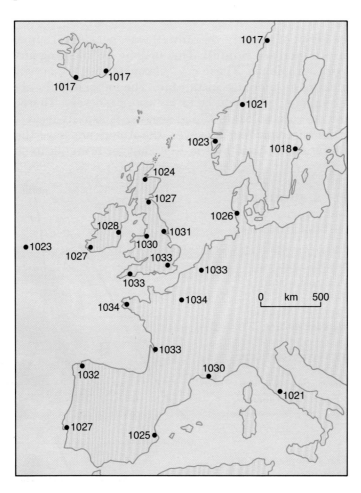

Figure 4.14 Atmospheric pressures in Europe measured on one day in February.

Exercise

1 Lay a piece of tracing paper over Figure 4.14 and, in pen, mark the places and write down their atmospheric pressure. Draw isobars at 4 mb (millibar) intervals beginning with 1032 mb. This line should enclose the places with a pressure greater than 1032 mb and it should go through the places with exactly that pressure. The next line to draw is 1028 mb, outside your first line. You will need to draw five lines altogether.

2 Is the pressure high or low in the centre of the isobar map you have drawn? Is rain likely in these conditions? Explain your answer.

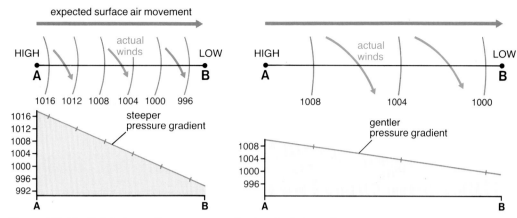

Figure 4.15 The link between the pressure gradient and wind speed.

The winds would be quite light on the day for which you have drawn a map. We can tell this by the spacing of the isobars. The distance apart of the isobars tells us the pressure gradient. Figure 4.15 explains what this means.

The wind will be blowing out from the centre of the high pressure in both cases, but where there is a steeper pressure gradient the air will move more quickly. (Imagine a car being allowed to free wheel down each slope.) But we also know that the rotation of the earth deflects the wind to the right, so it does not blow straight from high to low, but more diagonally. This saying might help you to remember this deflection. 'If you stand with your back to the wind in the northern hemisphere, the *Low* pressure centre will be on your *Left.*'

On your pressure map, now draw the direction in which you think the wind will blow.

High pressure systems are usually welcome because they bring fine, calm weather, especially in summer. In 1976 these high pressure conditions brought extreme weather to Britain.

The 1975/1976 drought: an extreme event

The period between May 1975 and August 1976 was the driest 16 months in the UK since records began in 1727. The map in Figure 4.2(b) on page 95 shows the amount of rain which fell in summer 1976 as a percentage of the average measured over the previous 30 years.

Exercise

1 Look at Figure 4.2(b). Which areas of Britain had the lowest percentage of their normal rainfall? What was this percentage? Which parts of Britain had a normal amount of rainfall?

Figure 4.16 on page 108 gives a clue about why rainfall was so low. It shows the frequency of *anticyclones* (high pressure systems) in the same period. Normally these high pressure centres are located over Southern Europe and the Mediterranean. What happened was that large, persistent blocking highs sat over Britain for much of this time period. Their presence meant that any low pressure systems approaching Britain were steered to the south or to the north, but were unable to cross Britain. In fact a lot of Mediterranean resorts had unusually high rainfall in spring and summer 1976 – rain that would normally have landed on us. It was also unusually hot during that summer. On every day from 23rd June – 7th July 1976 a maximum temperature of 32°C was recorded somewhere in the UK.

2 Explain why it was also likely to become very hot during the dry summer.

3 Why was convectional rainfall not formed? (Consider carefully what is needed for rain to form, and look back to the section on convectional rainfall on p. 103.)

4 Study the maps in Figure 4.17 and describe some of the consequences of the drought. Make sure you describe where these consequences were most serious, and try to explain why this was so.

5 Although not hardest hit by the drought, Wales suffered the greatest shortages of water for domestic supply. Find out why this was so. It will help you to know that several reservoirs in Wales supply English cities with water.

6 Consider who might have benefitted from the unusual weather conditions in the summer of 1976.

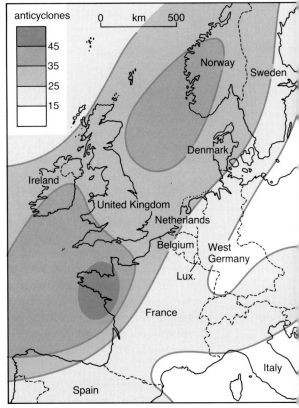

Figure 4.16 The frequency of anticyclones over north west Europe between May 1975 and August 1976.

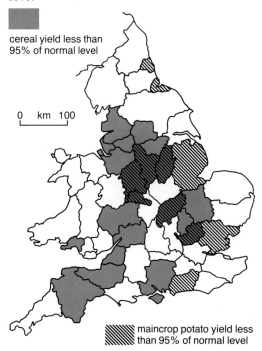

Figure 4.17 Some effects of the 1976 drought in Britain:
(a) The reduction in the yield of cereals and maincrop potatoes during 1976. The yield in 1976 has been worked out as a percentage of the yield in 1974, an average year. Those counties where the yield was 95% or less of the normal yield are shaded.

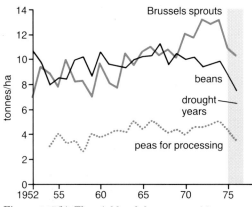

Figure 4.17(b) The yields of three vegetable crops in the UK.

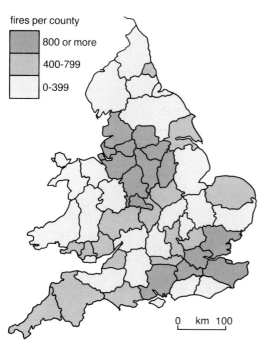

Figure 4.17(c) The frequency of grassland fires between June and August, 1976.

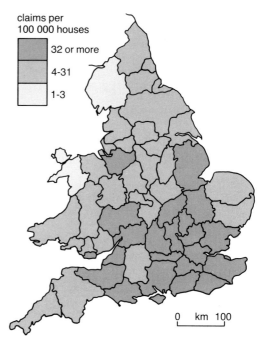

Figure 4.17(d) The number of claims made by people suffering subsidence damage in 1976.

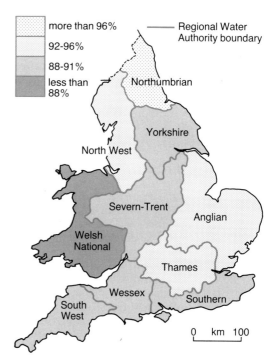

Figure 4.17(e) Water supply in 1976 as a percentage of average supply.

High pressure systems in winter

In winter, high pressure systems are not so popular, as they can mean frost and fog.

Frost

Figure 4.18 shows why high pressure systems can cause frost. High pressure means descending air, and fewer clouds. It also means that there are only light winds or even still air. At night there is no blanket to keep the earth's heat in, so it escapes, and the ground can become very cold.

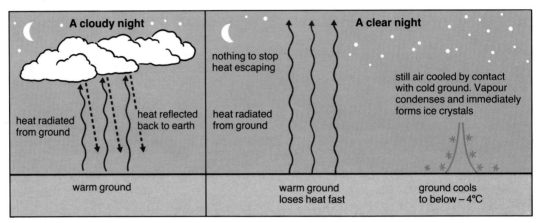

Figure 4.18 The conditions likely to cause frost to form.

Frost is more likely at the bottom of a slope, rather than on the slope. You ought to be able to explain why – think about what happens to cold air. This explains why fruit farmers prefer to plant their fruit trees on a slope rather than at the bottom of it.

Exercise

1 Look at Figure 4.19 which shows the number of air frosts each month in 1987 in Aviemore, Lowestoft and Valentia.
   a) How many frost free months were there in Aviemore?
   b) Which of the three towns experienced fewest frosts in 1987?
   c) Explain why this town has fewest frosts. You will need to mention its position at the coast, the North Atlantic Drift, the wind direction, and its latitude. Look back at the section on temperature before you write.

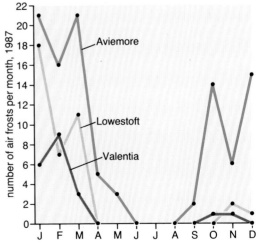

Figure 4.19 A comparison of the number of air frosts in Aviemore, Lowestoft and Valentia.

Fog

Fog is another type of weather linked to high pressure conditions. Three conditions are needed for fog to form –

- The air must be fairly still.
- The sky must be clear, so that ground cools quickly at night.
- The air must be moist – ie. containing a lot of water vapour.

The cold ground will chill the air next to it, and some of the vapour in the air will condense into droplets.

Exercise

1 Draw a diagram to show the conditions necessary for the formation of fog. Add labels to show the processes which are occurring.

The effects of air pollution on fog and rain

The process of fog formation is helped by the presence of smoke and dust particles in the air. In December 1952, London was hit by a deadly smog which lay over the city for a week. The smog contained large amounts of smoke and sulphur dioxide, and was very acid, possibly with a pH of 1.6. (That is more acid than lemon juice.) About 4000 people died from various bronchial complaints, and even from heart attacks as they fought for breath.

This smog was so serious that a number of Clean Air Acts were passed. These banned the burning of smoky fuels in cities.

Exercise

Look at Figure 4.20(a) which shows smoke concentrations and number of days with fog and thick fog in Oxford.

1 Does there seem to be a link between the occurrence of fog and the amount of smoke in the air? What is the link?

Figure 4.20(a) Smoke concentration and the occurrence of fog in Oxford, 1959–1978.

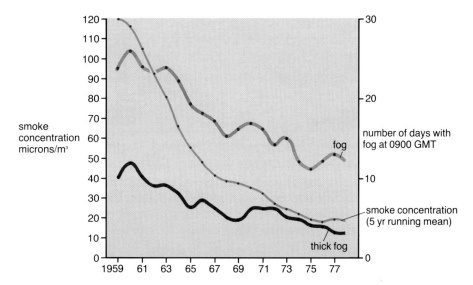

Figure 4.20(b) Fog at Fiddler's Ferry, North Seaton.

The reason for the decline in the number of fogs in Oxford was not just the setting up of smokeless zones. There was also a change to more convenient fuels like oil and gas for home heating, instead of coal. Since more women went out to work, fires weren't kept burning all day. The town gas works was closed in 1960, and steam trains stopped running in 1965.

Sulphur dioxide – another polluter of the atmosphere – has *not* been banned. In the 1970s power stations were pumping more than five million tonnes of sulphur dioxide into the air over Europe every year. Not only that, but chimney stacks were built much taller; the highest one is 259 m high. Previously the smoke and gases landed fairly close to the industries, because they weren't put high into the air. (Figure 4.21.) Pollution was a local problem. Now the pollution gets higher

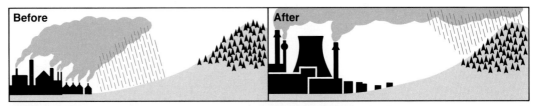

Figure 4.21 The extent of air pollution from power stations, in the past and today.

into the atmosphere, and is carried away by the wind. Local conditions have improved but the problem has moved further afield. Rain with sulphur dioxide dissolved in it (acid rain) is a global problem. Canada blames the USA, Norway blames Britain and acid rain damage is reported as far apart as Australia, Mexico and China. There are three things we can do about this:

1 Sulphur can be removed from power station emissions (outputs) using limestone.

2 Catalytic converters can be added to car exhaust systems to remove hydro-carbons and nitrogen oxide.
3 Dumping large quantities of limestone in soils and water masses will reduce acidity. Adding fertilisers and nutrients to forest soils will also help.

The problem of acid rain and its effect on ecosystems is dealt with more fully on page 157.

Low pressure systems

Exercise

Figure 4.22 shows a typical low pressure system centred to the north west of Britain on 19 and 20 November.

1 See how much you can work out about the weather from this map. Find Valentia in South West Ireland and note down five facts about the weather conditions there at 06.00 hours on 20 November.

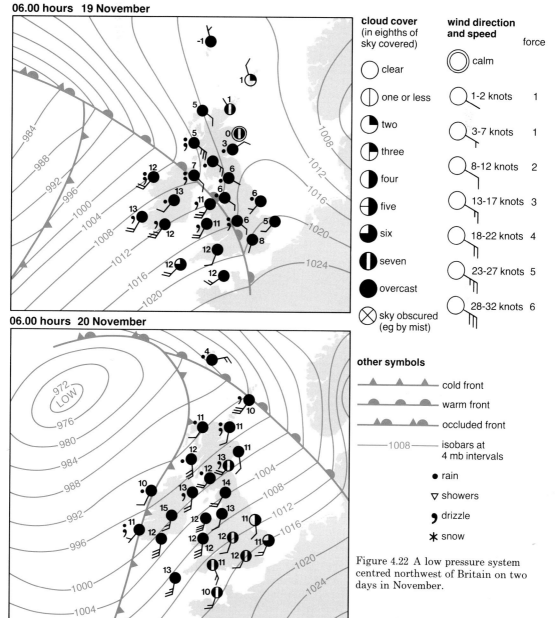

Figure 4.22 A low pressure system centred northwest of Britain on two days in November.

How did this low pressure system develop? It began as a small wave on the boundary between a warm air mass and a cold air mass (Figure 4.23). The warm air is approaching from the south west, and the cold air from the north east. As the warm air pushes up against the cold air, it is the warm air that is forced to rise. This boundary is called the *warm front*. Clouds form along the front as the warm air cools and condensation takes place.

At the *cold front*, cold air is being pushed into the warm air mass, and almost bulldozing the warm air mass off the ground. This cold front is a steeper boundary as you can see in the cross section.

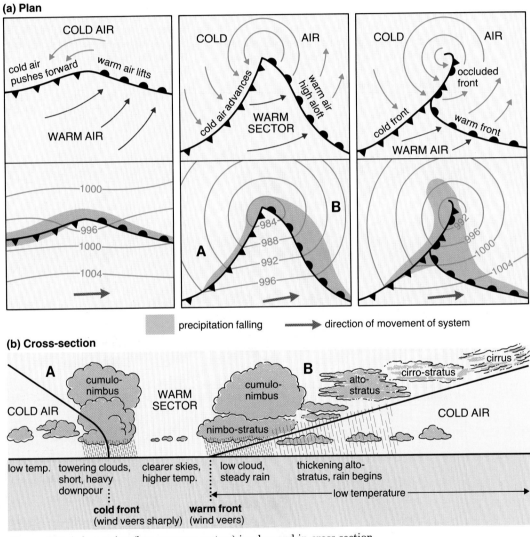

Figure 4.23 A depression (low pressure system) in plan and in cross section.

2 Find Lowestoft in East Anglia and note down four changes in its weather over the 24 hour period beginning 06.00 hours on 19 November.

3 Describe what happens to the position of the warm front in these 24 hours.

Exercise

Use all the information in Figure 4.22 and 4.23 to answer the following questions.

1 Why is the temperature in East Anglia colder than the temperature in Cornwall at 06.00 hours on 19 November?

2 What would you expect to happen to the temperature in Ireland later on 20 November as the cold front passes over?

3 When can the people in Birmingham expect the next period of heavy rain?

4 Where are the skies clearest on 20 November? Why is there less cloud in these places?

Low pressure systems like this are very common over Britain. Occasionally they develop into very deep depressions, with extremely low pressure in their centre. One such storm occurred on the night of 15/16th October 1987.

The Great Storm of October 1987

This was one of the most severe storms ever experienced in Britain, and was described by some newspapers as a hurricane. There certainly were hurricane-force winds at some places. Use the newspaper extract in Figure 4.24 to work out some of the details of the storm.

The timetable of havoc in Britain's worst storm

The most violent storm ever recorded in Britain was almost completely unpredicted in public weather forecasts, the Meteorological Office admitted yesterday. Had it struck in daylight, with many people out of doors, the consequences could have been disastrous (Robin Young writes).

The main evening forecast at 9.30 pm on Thursday predicted 30 mph winds, with gusts up to 50 mph. The midnight forecast on Radio 4 did warn of a risk of serious gales, but it was an hour before the Met Office alerted fire brigades and police forces to the danger of extreme winds.

A Meteorological Office spokesman said yesterday: "We had forecast the risk of very high winds at the end of the week as long ago as last Sunday, but we did fail to fill in the detail. The storm blew up over the Bay of Biscay and came in over the sea from an area where we have very very sparse weather information. We failed to realize the rapid way in which the depression was deepening."

The cause of the storm was a collision between a belt of very warm humid air drawn up from the west of Africa and cold Arctic air drawn down over the Atlantic. The resultant depression, the deepest recorded in Britain, deepened rapidly, passing west of the Brest peninsula and the Channel Islands before centring over England in the small hours of the morning.

The strongest winds were the southerlies and south-westerlies blowing at the centre of the storm as it travelled from Devon to Humberside. Gusts of more than 100 miles per hour were recorded in the Isle of Wight and along the South Coast, and of 110 mph in Guernsey. In London the wind gusted up to 94 mph, the highest since records began in 1940. The fiercest gust at Heathrow reached 93 mph, 30 mph faster than anything previously recorded there. The highest mean speed recorded was at Manston in Kent, where over ten minutes the wind averaged 69 mph, only 4 mph short of the speed for an officially designated hurricane on the Beaufort scale.

● Britain's worst gale was the great Channel storm of November 26 and 27, 1703, which ravaged southern England and was estimated to have killed about 8,000 people. Thousands of tons of shipping were lost and the first Eddystone lighthouse was destroyed.

Figure 4.24(a) The Great October Gale, 1987. *The Times* 17.10.87

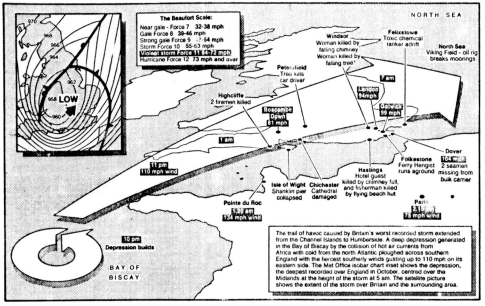

Figure 4.24(b) A newspaper report on the trail of havoc caused by the October 1987 storm. *The Times* 17.10.87

Exercise

1 On an outline map of Britain mark the places mentioned in the article on page 115 where there was damage or loss of life. Add the following places to the map:

> Chatham, Kent (three died as a house collapsed and trees fell).
> Benenden, Kent (man killed in home).
> Sevenoaks, Kent (six of seven historic oaks uprooted).
> Rottingdene, Sussex (elderly man killed in home).
> Selsea, Sussex (mobile homes overturned).
> Harwich, Suffolk (ferry adrift).

2 Add to your outline map, the centre of the storm at 22.00 hours, 23.00 hours, 01.00 hours, and 07.00 hours. Mark the path of the storm with a wide arrow.

3 How long did the storm take to cross Britain? Work out the distance it covered, and the speed at which it must have travelled. (Remember, speed = distance divided by time).

4 Find out from the extract why the depression formed and became so deep.

5 Why were the meteorological office unable to forecast how serious the storm would be?

6 Why might the consequences of the storm have been worse if it had occurred in the daytime instead of at night?

7 Storms more intense than this have occurred in the Scottish mountains. In the winter of 1981 there were winds of 140 mph in the Cairngorms. Why do we hear less about these storms, and much more about the October gale?

Snow

Snowfall is an aspect of Britain's weather about which we have mixed feelings. It is a fairly unusual occurrence. Figure 4.25(a) shows the median (or average) number of mornings on which we can expect to find snow.

Similar requirements are needed for snow to fall as for rain to fall, that is –

- Air is made to rise, at a front or over hills.
- Air must contain vapour.
- Air must be cold (but not too cold or it cannot hold much vapour).

Snow hazards have already been described in the section on temperature (page 100). An inch or so of snow can bring a British city to a halt, because we are not

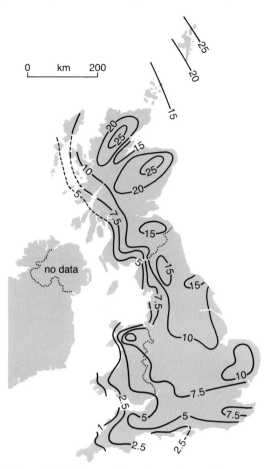

Figure 4.25(a) The number of mornings with snow lying in an average year in Britain.

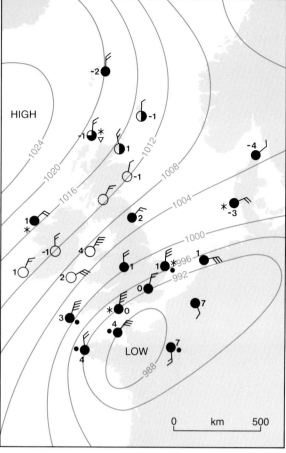

(b) The weather map for 0700 hrs. on Boxing Day, 1927, the day of the 'Christmas Blizzard'.

Exercise

Look at Figures 4.25(a) and (b) and use them to answer these questions.

1 In what parts of Britain is snow most likely to occur?

2 Why is snow so unlikely in Cornwall and West Wales? Give at least three reasons – referring back to the sections on temperature and rainfall.

3 Describe the weather situation on the East Coast of Britain on Boxing Day December 1927. Why were conditions suitable for snowfall?

used to the conditions, but in Canada, Norway, Sweden and the USSR for example, snow is a fact of life for much of the winter.

Tropical cyclones

Although some newspapers referred to the great October gale as a hurricane, that word was not really appropriate. A hurricane is a tropical storm in the Caribbean. In Asia these tropical storms are called *typhoons*. They are similar to our gale though, as they are all deep depressions with strong winds and heavy rain.

Tropical cyclones (see Figure 4.26(a)) usually occur at the end of the summer when the ocean is warmest. This means that the air above the ocean is likely to rise. As this warm, moist air rises condensation occurs. This releases *latent heat* (the heat that was originally used to evaporate the water). This heat makes the centre of the storm warmer, and in the eye of the storm warm dry air sinks, expands and sucks up more moisture to be carried upwards again.

The warm ocean 'feeds' the cyclone which becomes more and more intense, with increasing wind speeds around the calm eye of the storm. The hurricane itself moves fairly slowly in the direction of the prevailing winds, ie. east to west.

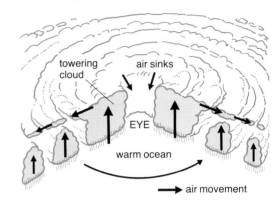

Figure 4.26(a) The structure of a hurricane.

As long as the cyclone keeps being supplied with moisture from the sea, and with heat from condensation, and as long as there is no friction at the surface, it will continue. Now you can see why most hurricanes will die as they cross land.

Figure 4.26(b) Hurricane David drives waves on shore in Puerto Rico.

Hurricane David, 1979

Exercise

Refer to Table 6 to answer these questions.

1 Use an atlas and an outline map of the world to mark Hurricane David's progress after its birth in the Sahara. Write the date next to each fixed position.

2 What happened to the wind speeds in the hurricane as it developed?

3 How far did it travel in its 12 day life? At what speed did it travel?

4 Look at Table 7 which shows reasons why few preparations were made for the disaster in Dominica. What could be done to ensure that people are better prepared in future?

Table 6   The life of Hurricane David, 1979

August 15–21	Sahara desert – dry hot air rising and colliding with moist cooler air from the equator. This is where the cyclone begins.
August 22	Trough passes Cape Verde Islands.
August 25	Trough becomes tropical depression, located 2500 km east of Windward Islands. Winds about 56 km/hour. Moving west at 30 km/hour.
August 26	Tropical depression gains strength from warm vapours of tropical waters. Wind speed 72 km/hour. Storm named David. Located 11.7°N, 45.5°W.
August 27	Eye has developed. Winds 120 km/hour so this is now classed as a hurricane. Position 1120km east of Lesser Antilles. At 12.00 hours Barbados issues hurricane watch.
August 28	09.00 hours, located at 13°N 56°W, winds 200 km/hour. 15.00 hours Dominica issues hurricane watch.
August 29	Hurricane hits Dominica by late morning. Winds 225 km/hour. 56 dead. Three quarters of the islanders are homeless.
August 30	Winds 240 km/hour. Hurricane crosses Puerto Rico's south coast. 13 die.
August 31	Hits Dominican Republic. Kills several hundred. Hurricane begins to lose strength as it hits the mountains and has no water to feed it.
September 1	Hurricane begins to die.

Table 7   Reasons why few preparations were made in Dominica:

1   Too little money available in the country.
2   People did not find out early enough about the hurricane.
3   There were no shelters available for people.
4   People did not remember the last big hurricane in the 1920s.
5   They thought the risk was fairly low.

Climate at the world scale

At the world scale, the climate is also controlled by the same major influences that were noted on page 95, ie. the radiation from the sun, and the atmospheric circulation. Look back to the simple world atmospheric circulation model on page 101. We can now add the type of temperature and rainfall conditions we would expect to find in each pressure belt.

Exercise

1 Copy Table 8. Use an atlas to complete approximate temperature details. As an example of each type of climate, you could look up the following parts of the world:

Polar – Spitsbergen, Greenland, Antarctica
Temperate – Britain, New Zealand
Sub-tropical – Sahara desert (Libya, Algeria), central Australia
Equatorial – Zaire, Malaysia, northern Brazil

If it is impossible to find figures to put into your table, words like hot, warm, mild, cold can be used to describe the temperature and very wet, wet, dry can be used to describe rainfall. You should notice on the atlas that the different climate zones are linked to the different air pressure belts.

Table 8

Climate type	Pressure conditions	Average temperature	Annual rainfall
Polar	High		
Temperate	Low		
Sub-tropical	High		
Equatorial	Low		

2 Make a large copy of Figure 4.27. Beneath it
  add the correct word to describe the climate
  type. The four words you need are in the
  first column of Table 8.

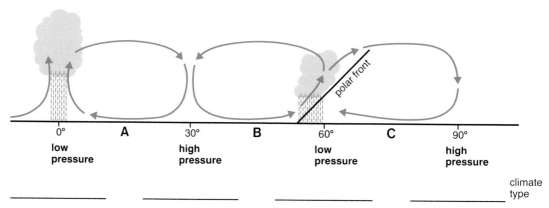

Figure 4.27 A simplified atmospheric circulation for one hemisphere.

The zones labelled A, B and C have a climate which is half of one major type
and half of another. In June all the world's pressure belts (and climate zones)
move north with the sun, and areas A, B and C have the climate normally found
to the south of them.

3 Redraw Figure 4.27 to show the position of   At what latitude will you now find:
  the pressure belts in June, when the sun   (a) the equatorial low pressure belt;
  shines directly on the Tropic of Cancer. The   (b) the sub-tropical high pressure belt;
  pressure belts move about 10°N at this time.   (c) the temperate low pressure belt?

In December the zones all move south, and the three areas A, B and C now have
the climate normally found to the north of them. Now you can work out what the
summer and winter seasons will be like in zones A, B and C. Copy and complete
Table 9.

Table 9

Area	Summer season	Winter season
A	Hot and wet	Warm and dry
B		
C		

Areas A, B and C therefore also have distinctive climates, with names you
might recognise. The areas between the equatorial low and the sub-tropical high
are the Savanna lands. Areas with climate B are the Mediterranean lands at
latitude 40°N and S.

4 Look at Table 10, showing climate statistics for two towns, one in the northern and one in the southern hemisphere. One has an A-type (Savanna) climate, the other a B-type (Mediterranean) climate. You have to decide which is which. To help you work this out, decide which is the warmest season in each place and add up the rainfall totals for the warmest six months. You might prefer actually to draw climate graphs for the two towns to compare them. Which town has a hot, wet summer and which a hot, dry one? The actual temperatures will also help you to decide which is which, as one town is at latitude 38°N and the other at latitude 12°S. Will the warmest one be nearest to or furthest from the equator? When you have decided which town has which type of climate, look up Darwin and Athens in an atlas. Now name Town 1 and Town 2.

Table 10

Town 1	J	F	M	A	M	J	J	A	S	O	N	D
Temp °C	9	9	12	15	19	24	27	27	24	20	15	11
Rain mm	56	41	36	20	20	15	5	10	15	43	71	71
Town 2	J	F	M	A	M	J	J	A	S	O	N	D
Temp °C	29	29	29	29	28	26	25	27	28	30	30	30
Rain mm	386	312	254	97	15	3	1	3	13	51	120	239

5 Why is the Mediterranean such a popular destination for tourists in the summer? Why would it not be as popular in December?

Later in this book you will learn more about life in two of the major climate types of the world – the equatorial climate and the polar climate. The way of life, the types of vegetation and farming, and all types of development are strongly affected by the climate of the area. You will need to look back to this section on climate when you start work on these two ecosystems.

Alterations to the global pattern

The earth's climates have changed over geological time. There have, for example, been ice ages, the effects of which are investigated on pages 83 to 85. These changes are very slow, lasting thousands of years, and they occur naturally. They are probably caused by alterations in the output of solar radiation, and changes in the earth's orbit.

1983 was a year of unusual weather. There were droughts in large parts of Africa, India, Australia and Indonesia, yet there were storms and floods in South America and Europe. Fisheries were destroyed and the bird population of Christmas Island, estimated at 17 000 000, disappeared. All of these occurrences could be linked to one extraordinary act of nature – the arrival of a warm current on South America's western coast. This current is called *El Nino*. *El Nino* means 'the child,' and the current is called this because it usually arrives off the coast of South America at Christmas time.

The El Nino *Current*

Every few years the surface waters of the Eastern Pacific Ocean become unusually warm. These waters are usually cold, but for some reason, warm water pushes eastwards over the cold water and piles up on the west coast of South America. The winds which normally blow south easterly slacken, and in 1983 they began to blow from the west. This helped the water to pile up on the coast of South America.

El Nino has had bad effects before. In 1972 its warm waters killed shoals of anchovy, and all but destroyed Peru's anchovy fishing industry. In 1983, *El Nino* raised water temperatures to 32°C in places off the coast of Peru, 7°C above normal. These warm waters are low in oxygen and nutrients, and are lethal to fish life.

Exercise

1 Look at Figure 4.28. Describe Peru's total
fish catch over the last 25 years. What
evidence is there that *El Nino* affects the fish
catch? Could anything else be responsible for
the remarkable decline in fishing since 1971?

Figure 4.28 The total Peruvian fish catch between
1961 and 1984.

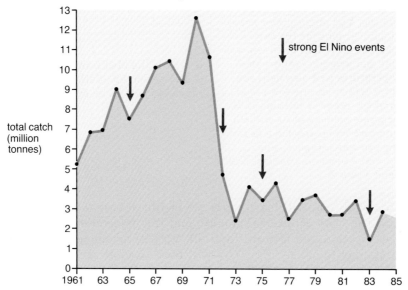

The warm waters also heat the lower atmosphere, and warm moist air arrives
on shore. This air rises over the coastal hills and mountains, and produces heavy
rainfall on bare, unvegetated land. (This land is normally very dry and con-
sequently very little grows) This causes catastrophic soil erosion and mud slides.

This example illustrates the fact that climates throughout the world are all
linked parts of one giant weather machine, and that a change in one part of the
system can have far reaching consequences.

2 Construct a flow diagram showing as many
as possible of the consequences of *El Nino* in
1983. Could anything be done to prevent any
of these consequences?

The greenhouse effect

Recently, scientists have become concerned about other changes to the world's
climates which are caused by human activity. One such change is the greenhouse
effect.

This is caused by carbon dioxide and other gases trapping the sun's heat within
the earth's atmosphere (Figure 4.29(a)). The world is already about 0.5°C warmer
than it was in the middle of the last century. 1981, 1983, and 1987 were all unusually warm years (they all also had more *El Nino* events). Some scientist are predicting that world temperatures will rise by 2°C by the year 2030. The question is,
what effect will this warming have on the climate? Figure 4.29(b) suggests some
changes, but few people are making firm predictions about what will happen – the
weather machine is too complex.

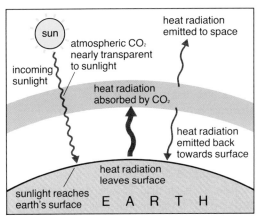

Figure 4.29 The greenhouse effect:
(a) its causes

Exercise

1 Look at the diagram in Figure 4.29(b) showing 'what could happen'. In each case suggest why that prediction has been made. Do these predictions seem rather far fetched?

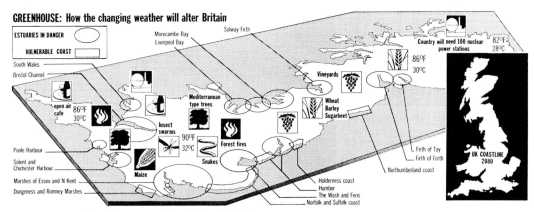

(b) and some of its effects as predicted by a British newspaper.

The ozone layer

Another serious concern is the *ozone layer*. In September 1987 scientists reported a hole in the ozone layer over Antarctica. It lasted from August until early December. This hole has received a great deal of publicity, and it is indeed potentially very dangerous.

The ozone layer is about 14–21 km above the earth's surface. In this layer, solar energy is absorbed, in particular the ultra-violet radiation from the sun. This ultra-violet radiation can be damaging to fisheries and crops and can cause skin cancer in humans. The loss of the ozone layer may also have consequences for the world's climate, but it is not clear what these might be.

Why does the hole appear each year?

The main reason is the use of *chlorofluorocarbons* (CFCs) in industrial societies. The CFCs react with ozone to break down the ozone layer.

Where do we use CFCs?

There are three main uses –

- As a propellant in all kinds of aerosols.
- In foam-blowing processes such as making take-away cartons, cavity wall insulation, fire fighting.
- As a coolant in refrigerators and air conditioners. Every time an old refrigerator is dumped, the CFCs leak into the atmosphere.

What can we do about this?

Governments can ban the use of CFCs in aerosols. The USA did this in the 1970s. Individual consumers like you can refuse to buy aerosols containing CFCs. Instead, look for ozone-friendly labels on products. Manufacturers need to look for alternative forms of packing, like cardboard eggboxes instead of blown foam ones. The campaign against CFCs is proving successful and a number of manufacturers, shops and services (like fast-food chains) have already changed to more environmentally friendly packaging.

Summary

1   As a summary to the work on weather and climate, have a go at the word-search in Figure 4.30. You should be able to find 26 words connected with weather and climate written frontwards, backwards and diagonally. At least ten of the words refer to weather hazards.

X	H	U	R	R	I	C	A	N	E	N
W	O	N	S	S	M	O	G	W	U	I
D	T	S	O	R	F	X	O	S	X	A
E	X	B	H	A	I	L	I	C	E	R
P	A	L	I	G	H	T	N	I	N	G
R	C	F	D	R	A	Z	Z	I	L	B
E	I	R	R	V	A	P	O	U	R	X
S	D	O	O	L	F	O	Z	O	N	E
S	A	N	U	O	R	E	L	I	E	F
I	I	T	G	T	H	U	N	D	E	R
O	R	X	H	E	A	T	W	A	V	E
N	O	I	T	A	I	D	A	R	X	X
A	N	T	I	C	Y	C	L	O	N	E

Figure 4.30 A wordsearch on weather and climate.

2   Consider Lake Michigan in the United States – a huge lake 500 km × 100 km (50 000 km^2). List some of the effects this lake might have on:
a)   summer temperatures;
b)   winter temperatures;
c)   rainfall;
d)   the likelihood of frost;
in the area surrounding the lake. In each case explain your reasoning carefully.

CHAPTER FIVE

Ecosystems

The part of the earth in which there is life – the water, the soil and the air – is called the *biosphere*. If you imagine the earth is an apple, then the biosphere would be as thin as the skin of the apple. However it is of vital importance to us because it is where we live.

We usually divide the biosphere into smaller chunks called *ecosystems*. An ecosystem is a more manageable unit to study. It is a set of inter-acting components (Figure 5.1), some of which are living and some non-living. The living parts of an ecosystem are *producers, consumers* and *decomposers*

Producers – these are the plants which make their own foods. They make them from:

- carbon dioxide taken in from the atmosphere through leaf walls;
- inorganic salts (phosphorous and nitrates) and water which are taken in from the soil via plant roots.

Plants use sunlight to convert water and carbon dioxide into starch and sugar. This process is called *photosynthesis* and only happens in plants which contain *chlorophyll*. (Chlorophyll is the green colouring matter of plants.)

Consumers – these cannot photosynthesise, so they cannot make their own food. There are two levels of consumers:

- herbivores which eat plants;
- carnivores which eat other animals.

Humans can eat both plants and animals.

Decomposers – these are the bacteria and fungi which break down dead plant and animal matter and animal waste, so that the *nutrients* (useful minerals) in them are released into the soil, water or air.

The non-living parts of the ecosystem are:

- Soil – broken down rock particles, plus decomposed and rotting plant and animal remains.
- Air – which contains important gases like oxygen, nitrogen, carbon dioxide.
- Water – which is often used to transport nutrients through the ecosystem.

The final, essential ingredient is the input of energy from outside the ecosystem – the sun. All of this is summarised in Figure 5.1 on the following page.

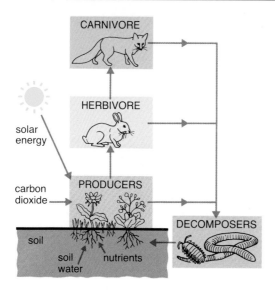

Figure 5.1 The main components of an ecosystem.

Exercise

1 Re-draw Figure 5.1 twice, leaving the boxes empty. Use the following words to illustrate two different ecosystems. You will need to separate the words into two groups, then decide which are producers, which are herbivores and so on. Name the two ecosystems which you have drawn.

Words (components of ecosystems) bacteria, plankton, fungi, human, kingfisher, sheep, minnow, grass.

Nutrients in the ecosystem

Nutrients are the things necessary for growth, such as carbon, hydrogen, oxygen, nitrogen, calcium, magnesium, potassium. Within every ecosystem nutrients are moving through the system. Where do these nutrients come from? Some come from the air. Others come from rock weathering. Decaying plants and animals provide some, and some are added artificially in fertilisers. Rainfall can also supply them.

Nutrients move through the ecosystem, often in water. They can also leave the ecosystem. For example, rainfall can wash the nutrients down through the soil and take them right out of one ecosystem. This process is called *leaching*. It happens particularly when the rainwater moving through the soil is acidic. When crops or animals are harvested, their remains cannot rot in the ecosystem, and the nutrients in them are lost.

Exercise

1 Imagine the following types of ecosystem:

– a wheatfield
– a field used for grazing a beef cattle herd
– a forest affected by acid rain, and used to provide sawn timber

For each one:
i) draw a simple diagram using Figure 5.2 as a basis to show the components of the ecosystem and the flows of nutrients;
ii) are any nutrients removed from the system? If so, when and how?
iii) What can be done in each case to re-place lost nutrients?

When drawing the wheatfield example you will only have producers (the wheat) in the biomass box, unless there are some mice getting at the crop!

The three stores hold a certain proportion of all the nutrients in the ecosystem at any time. In different ecosystems, the stores have a different importance. Figure 5.3 compares nutrient cycling in a temperate deciduous forest like Sherwood Forest, and a tropical rain forest like Amazonia. The sizes of the circles show the importance of the three different stores. The width of the arrow shows the quantity of nutrients in that flow.

2 Which store holds most nutrients in both ecosystems?

3 In which ecosystem are the soil and litter stores least important?

4 When nutrients reach the soil store in the tropical rain forest, what happens to them? (Do they stay there or do they move on?)

5 In one of these ecosystems the nutrient flows are larger than the stores. The nutrients are being cycled very quickly. Which ecosystem is it?

6 If the living matter (*biomass*) is removed from the tropical rain forest, what effect would it have on the amount of nutrients left in the system?

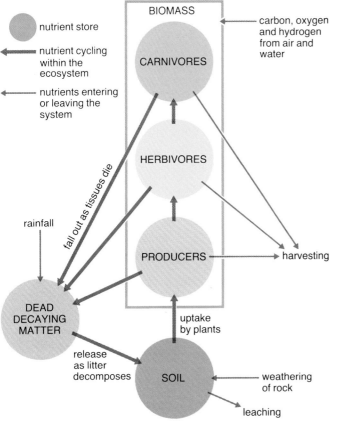

Figure 5.2 Nutrient cycling in an ecosystem.

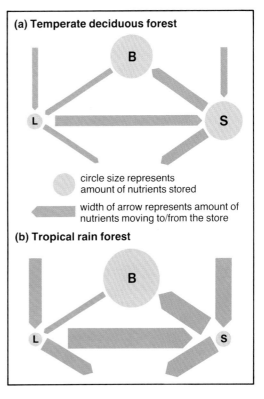

Figure 5.3 A comparison of the nutrients flowing through the ecosystem and those held in the stores, in two sorts of forest.

Humans can have a big impact on nutrient cycling, in natural and farming ecosystems. We have already seen how cutting timber removes plant material and nutrients from a forest ecosystem. Farming ecosystems can be balanced as long as nutrients are returned to the land, as we shall see later in this chapter.

Soil

Soil is one of the non-living, but essential, components of an ecosystem. It provides necessary water and nutrients, and a firm foothold for the plants to grow from. It has basically four constituents, shown in Figure 5.4(a). Study this diagram very carefully. Figure 5.4(b) shows where these four constituents come from, and Figure 5.4(c) gives some more details of the importance of each constituent.

Clay and humus are obviously very important to soils. They are important because:

- they can hold water
- they can store plant nutrients
- they give the soil a good structure by helping the particles to clump together into 'crumbs'.

Figure 5.4 Three aspects of soil:

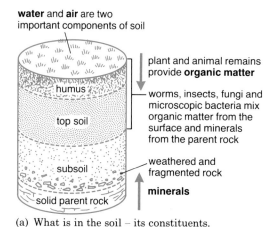

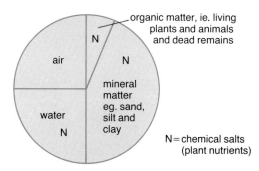

(b) The importance of the four soil constituents in a typical British farm soil.

(a) What is in the soil – its constituents.

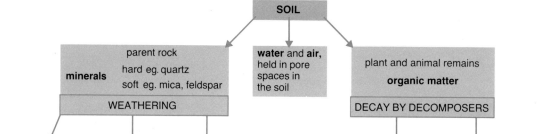

(c) The sources of the soil constituents.

Exercise

Use Figure 5.4(a), (b) and (c) to answer these questions.

1 In Britain, what is the largest constituent of the soil? Where does it come from?

2 How does the organic matter reach the soil? Approximately what percentage of the soil mass does it form?

3 How do the minerals and the humus (decayed vegetation) get mixed in the soil?

4 How do important plant nutrients like calcium, potassium and nitrogen get into the soil?

5 Which two components of the soil are important for storing these nutrients in the soil?

6 What would a soil without any humus or any clay be like?

Soil structure

The *structure* of the soil is the size of the clumps in the soil. It affects the availability of air and water in the soil. It also affects the chance of the soil being eroded. Where the spaces between the clumps are minute (*micropores*), water can be held there by suction (Figure 5.5(a)). Since the water fills the spaces, there is less air in the soil. *Macropores* are bigger and let water flow down through them easily, so the spaces can usually be filled with air (Figure 5.5(b)). A loamy soil has a good mixture of clay, sand, silt and humus. It has a crumb structure with macropores to give room in the soil for air, and micropores for water to be stored in (Figure 5.5(c)).

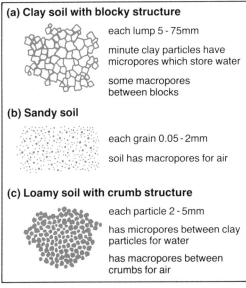

(a) Clay soil with blocky structure

each lump 5 - 75mm

minute clay particles have micropores which store water

some macropores between blocks

(b) Sandy soil

each grain 0.05 - 2mm

soil has macropores for air

(c) Loamy soil with crumb structure

each particle 2 - 5mm

has micropores between clay particles for water

has macropores between crumbs for air

Figure 5.5 Three contrasting soil structures.

Exercise

1 Which of the three soils in Figure 5.5 is most likely to become waterlogged?

2 Which of the three soils would need most watering to keep the crops growing in a dry spell? Why?

3 Sandy soils are often preferred for market gardening because they warm up quickly in the spring. Why do they warm up quickly?

4 Root crops have to develop downwards through the soil. In which of the three soils would this be most difficult?

5 What could a farmer do to improve:
a) a sandy soil; or
b) a clay soil with a blocky structure.

A good soil structure is vital in protecting against soil erosion. Unfortunately it is all too easy to destroy the soil structure, and the price is now being paid in many areas of the world, such as Ethiopia, Nepal, Britain and the USA (see pages 132–138 for more detail).

Damaging the soil structure

How can the soil structure be broken down? There are four main ways in which this can happen.

a) *By reducing the amount of humus and organic matter in the soil*

The two exercises on page 130 illustrate the ways in which farming *can* reduce nutrient levels in the soil. Without the humus there is nothing in the soil to hold the mineral nutrients, to hold water, and to maintain the soil structure. The soil is then open to erosion.

b) *By ploughing*

Heavy farm machinery compresses the soil and can damage its structure, particularly when the soil is wet. The sole of the plough compresses the sub-soil, while leaving the surface loose. Repeated ploughing to the same depth will increase the density of the lower layer. The loose surface layers of the soil are then exposed to the sun and air. This allows the nutrients in the soil to be oxidised and lost as water washes them out.

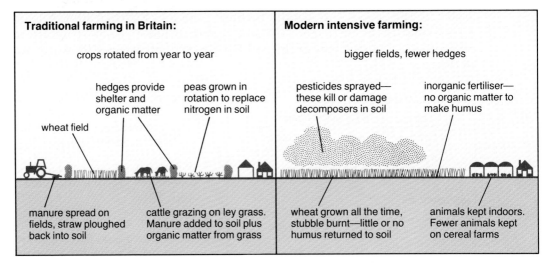

Figure 5.6 Some of the reasons for the reduction in the humus and organic matter in the soil caused by modern farming.

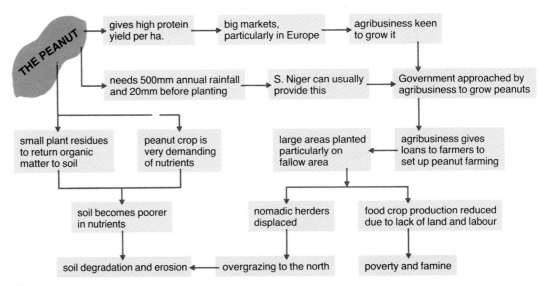

Figure 5.7 Consequences of peanut cultivation in Niger.

Exercise

1 Use Figure 5.6 to list the sources of humus and organic matter which *were* put into the soil using traditional farming methods, but are no longer used.

2 Look at Figure 5.7 which shows the effects of peanut cultivation in Niger in Africa. Give three reasons why growing peanuts on a large scale reduces the level of nutrients in the soil.

3 Why did overgrazing occur in northern Niger? In what way was it linked to the growing of peanuts in the south?

c)   By leaching

Rainwater is naturally slightly acid with a pH of about 5. It is slightly acid because of the gases dissolved in it, such as carbon dioxide. When this acid water moves down through the soil some of the nutrients (like calcium and magnesium) attached to the clay particles are dislodged. This removal of nutrients is called *leaching*. The nutrients are replaced by hydrogen ions which are left behind on the clay particles. The nutrients become soluble and are taken away in the rain-water. Now instead of the nutrients being attached to the clay particles, there is a lot of hydrogen. This makes the soil more acid. The clay particles are now less able to clump together and the structure breaks down.

Leaching is most likely when:
a) the rainfall is more acidic;
b) the rainwater can drain quickly through the soil carrying the minerals with it;
c) the rainfall is heavier;
d) the humus is acid, eg. under coniferous trees.

d) By fire

Fire has long been used by humans to control vegetation. In the tropical rain-forest, the shifting cultivators cut down trees and burnt the leaves and branches. The ashes produced a fertiliser containing nutrients which could be used by crops very quickly. However, the fire also destroyed a lot of organic matter which could have decomposed and released its nutrients more slowly. It also destroyed beneficial bacteria.

Burning is also widely used to destroy old, woody plant growth. In its place grow new juicy green shoots for animals to graze on. Much of the heather moor-land of upland Britain is the result of regular burning. Heather is a valuable forage plant for grouse and hill sheep. It is burned to keep as much as possible of the heather at its most productive stage – with a high proportion of edible green shoots. Heather is able to survive burning. Other grasses, shrubs and trees which might otherwise grow on these moorlands are killed off by burning. We therefore have large expanses of heather-covered moorland.

Exercise

1 What or who is controlling the burned heather moorland ecosystem? Why is it controlled?

2 What else, apart from plant variety, is lost from a burned heather moorland ecosystem?

Soil erosion

Exercise

1 Use all the evidence in Figures 5.6, 5.7 and 5.8 to show where the soil cycle can be inter-rupted and how the soil structure can be broken down.

2 For each of the following events, note down and explain which parts of the soil system (A, B, C, D, E, F in Figure 5.8) it would af-fect and what the knock-on effect might be:
a) creating a coniferous forest plantation for harvesting in forty years;
b) spraying pesticides on a cereal crop;
c) burning stubble instead of ploughing straw back into the soil;
d) rainfall becoming more acid as a result of air pollution;
e) intensive cereal farming instead of mixed arable and animal farming.

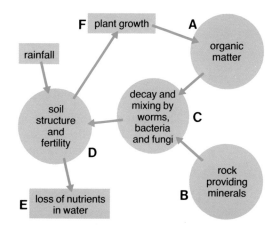

Figure 5.8 The soil cycle, showing how nutrients move through the soil.

In each of these cases something happens to interrupt or upset the soil ecosystem.

The result of any breakdown of the soil in these ways is soil erosion, by both wind and water.

Soil erosion case studies

It is difficult to give accurate estimates of soil erosion over large areas, but some think that by the year 2000, at least 275 billion tonnes of soil will have been lost. More than half of this total will have been lost from the United States, the Soviet Union, China and India. At the same time, the world population will probably be over six thousand million, compared with five thousand million today. So there will be an extra one thousand million people to feed, but less of the good farmland which is needed to feed them. And the year 2000 is less than 4000 days away! So soil erosion is one of the major problems the world faces. The following case studies illustrate some of the effects of soil erosion throughout the world.

'A land farmed into the ground' – Britain.

This description was used as the title for an article which appeared in *The Guardian* in December 1987. These are some of the facts recorded in the article:

1   Soil is created at about 0.5 tonnes per ha per year.
2   Soil losses on the South Downs in autumn 1987 were often over 30 tonnes per ha.
3   One field experienced a record loss of 270 tonnes per ha over 9 hectares.
4   Soil 100 cm deep sown with winter wheat yields 5 tonnes per ha.
    Soil 25 cm deep sown with winter wheat yields 3 tonnes per ha.
5   On 7 October, 80 houses in Rottingdean were affected by soil-laden water. A million pounds-worth of damage was done.
6   Brighton Borough Council spent £100 000 on protection for houses – trenches across hillsides, a major dam in front of some houses, 28 minor dams up the valley.

Exercise

1 a) What do facts 1, 2 and 3 tell you about the comparative rates of soil creation and soil loss? In other words, is soil in this area created more rapidly than it is lost?

b) What is the importance of fact 4? (Think about what is happening to the soil and how this will affect the farmer.)
c) What are some of the financial consequences of soil erosion? (Facts 4, 5 and 6.)

Several reasons are given for the soil erosion described in this article:

• The high price of wheat and EEC subsidies encourage farmers to grow wheat, even on thin soils and steep slopes.
• More winter wheat is being grown now, instead of spring wheat. This means that in the autumn and winter the ground is bare, and heavy autumn rain can erode it more easily.
• Farmers have created larger fields by pulling up the hedges which used to act as natural barriers to soil erosion.
• Farmers have been ploughing up and down the slopes rather than along the contour lines.

Albourne, West Sussex

John Boardman visited a strawberry field at Albourne in April 1980 and saw sand deposits about 10 cm deep at the bottom of the slope, covering part of the strawberry crop. Several reasons were given for this soil erosion.

1 Before 1962 there were five fields. Gradually the hedges and drains were removed until today there is one large field. (Figure 5.9(a).) It has different crops in different parts of the field, but there are no proper field boundaries. There is now one long slope, about 335 metres long, which drops about 16 metres. Previously this slope was divided into sections by hedges. (Figure 5.9(b).)

2 The strawberry crop does not cover and protect the soil very quickly. Raindrops splash onto the bare soil and dislodge particles. When straw was spread on and between the ridges the following year, there were fewer signs of soil erosion.

3 The soil contains a high proportion of fine sand and silt, so that soil particles are easily detached.

4 The furrows in the field run down the slope, so that water, carrying soil particles with it, can move downhill fairly easily. 146 furrows were counted leading down to the sand deposits at the bottom of the hill.

5 Rainfall in December 1979 was heavier than usual, and there were more days with over 7.5 millimetres of rain. This amount of rainfall is thought to be important in causing erosion.

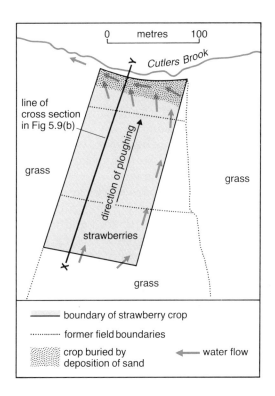

Figure 5.9(a) A plan of a strawberry field affected by soil erosion at Albourne in West Sussex.

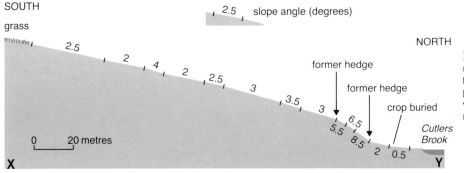

Figure 5.9(b) A cross section of the strawberry field, showing the positions of hedges which have been removed.

Exercise

1 Three of these causes of erosion are a result of human activity, one is natural but could be altered, and one is beyond our control. Which is which?

2 Thinking of your answers to question 1, what do you suggest this farmer could do to prevent soil erosion in future? Try to give three or four suggestions.

The Kleenex trail, Nepal

This was the title of a television programme describing the tourist route up the Khumbu Valley in Nepal towards Everest. It was so named because the route was littered with pink toilet paper, showing the lack of toilet facilities in the area. However, the worst effect of the tourists on the environment is the effect on forests.

Forests used to cover the valley slopes. Now there is little left. Why? About 15 000 tourists each year trek through the Khumbu Valley. They stay in lodges which have to use wood for heating and cooking for the tourists. Each lodge uses about 220 kg of wood each day in the high season. In one village alone – Namche Bazar – there are 20 lodges.

The tourists want hot showers after a hard day's trek. In Namche and Tengboche wood is burnt to heat water for hot showers. Campers staying in the higher parts of the valley are supposed to carry enough kerosene for all their cooking and water heating needs. They don't always do this, and the sherpa guides still cut wood.

Once damaged, it is hard to encourage the forest to re-grow. Young trees need the protection of larger trees if they are to be able to grow in this harsh environment.

The bare slopes are now a severe soil erosion risk. Not only can the soil be carried away forming gullies or landslides, but the rivers in the valley bottom become choked with soil, and therefore flood more easily.

Some steps are being taken to prevent this situation becoming worse. Part of the area where trees still grow has been designated as the Sargarmartha National Park, and the cutting down of live trees there is illegal. Micro hydro-electric schemes have been set up in Namche and Tengboche. The electricity they generate can be used for heating and cooking instead of fuel wood.

Figure 5.10 Deforestation for agriculture in Nepal.

Exercise

1 Draw a flow diagram showing the sequence of events which leads to soil erosion in the Khumbu Valley. Begin with the tourists.

2 Add a sequence of events to your diagram showing any possible benefits of the tourist industry.

3 Could any these benefits be used to improve the environmental problems?

A second example from a different part of South East Asia illustrates another effect of deforestation and soil erosion. The graph in Figure 5.11(a) shows the storage capacity of a reservoir in Andhra Pradesh in South India. The dam was built in 1930, and was designed to irrigate 0.11 million ha of farm land. It has since filled up with silt carried from the surrounding slopes, and in fact the reservoir once dried up completely in 1973 because of a drought. Figure 5.11(b) illustrates some of the reason why it silted up so rapidly.

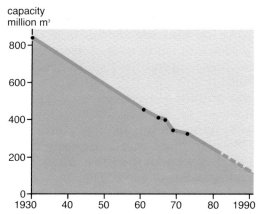

Figure 5.11(a) Loss of storage capacity in the Nizamsagar reservoir in Andhra Pradesh, India.

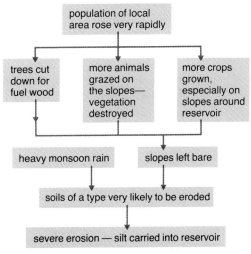

Figure 5.11(b) Causes of the silting up of the Nizamsagar reservoir.

Exercise

1 By how much has the capacity of the reservoir fallen already? Give your answer in cubic metres (m³).

2 If silting-up continues at the same rate, what might the life of this reservoir be? (ie. how many years will it take to become unusable?)

3 Was the silting-up of the reservoir preventable? If so, how? Base your answer on the flow diagram in Figure 5.11.

The Dust Bowl, USA

John Steinbeck wrote his novel *The Grapes of Wrath* in the 1930s. It describes graphically the effects of drought on a community of small tenant farmers in Oklahoma. Soil erosion on a large scale produced dust storms, which buried buildings as the dry soil was carried off and dropped elsewhere. These two short extracts from *The Grapes of Wrath* describe the effects of the dust.

'When the night came again it was black night, for the stars could not pierce the dust to get down, and the window lights could not even spread beyond their own yards. Now the dust was evenly mixed with the air, an emulsion of dust and air. Houses were shut tight, and cloth wedged around doors and windows, but the dust came in so thinly that it could not be seen in the air, and it settled like pollen on the chairs and table, on the dishes. The people brushed it from their shoulders. Little lines of dust lay at the door sills.'

'In the morning the dust hung like fog, and the sun was as red as ripe new blood. All day the dust sifted down from the sky and the next day it sifted down. An even blanket covered the earth. It settled on the corn, piled up on the tops of the fence posts, piled up on the wires; it settled on roofs, blanketed the weeds and trees.'

Soil erosion has continued to be a problem. It has been estimated that Iowa has lost half of its top soil in the last 200 years, and Kansas has lost 30% of its soil-borne nitrogen and 30% of its organic matter in the last 30 years.

In 1988 another major drought struck the USA. This drought has been blamed on the greenhouse effect (see page 122). However, the cause seems to be the same weather conditions that occurred in Britain in 1976. A large ridge of high pressure stuck over the USA. Rain-bearing low pressure systems from the west were diverted north over the Canadian prairies, or south over Mexico. This sort of 'blocking' by a high pressure system does happen from time to time, although the reasons for it are not well understood.

In parts of North Dakota there was no rain between August 1987 and July 1988. Snowfall in the Rockies was half the average. Not only did the crops fail, but the River Mississippi fell to 80% below its normal level, and forest fires affected several states including Montana, Missouri and Georgia. However the effects on the farmers were not as disastrous as they were in the 1930s. Much of the land is farmed by huge companies who own thousands of acres. They have been promised the same subsidy payments from the Government as they would have got if they had produced their crop.

Last year, many farms produced a surplus of wheat, which has been stored in silos. This wheat is now fetching a very high price, as it is in short supply.

Exercise

1 Draw a sketch outline of North America. Label Canada, USA and Mexico. Mark in the places mentioned above. Draw in the Mississippi river. Mark the position of the blocking high pressure and show with arrows where the westerly air flow has taken the rain.

2 Why has this drought not caused as much hardship and poverty as the one in the 1930s?

Overgrazing in Ethiopia

Exercise

Figure 5.12 shows the previous way of life of pastoral farmers such as the Afar, and how it was affected by the development of irrigated farming.

1 Explain why the pastoral farmers moved their herds twice a year.

2 How were the ways of life of the herders and the settled farmers linked?

3 What disrupted this system?

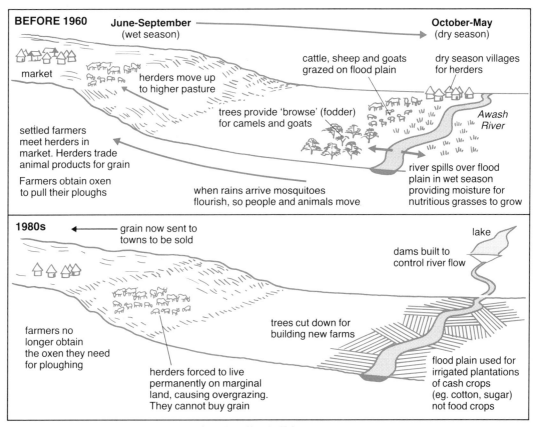

Figure 5.12 Changes in land use in the Awash valley in Ethiopia.

Now that people like the Afar in Ethiopia are forced to live on the drier lands where there is not enough grazing, they suffer more when there is a drought. It has been estimated that the 1972–73 drought caused a famine in which 25–30% of the Afar may have died. Previous droughts could be survived because the Afar could use the river floodplain and they could still buy grain locally. In other words a drought does not necessarily cause a famine. Some people have gone as far as saying that the 1973 and 1984 famines were the result of human activity.

In all these examples, there is a common pattern explaining why soil erosion occurred, which is summarised in Figure 5.13. This sequence of events must be interrupted, to reverse the processes. The list on page 138 gives some suggestions about how to do this.

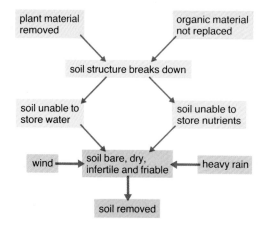

Figure 5.13(a) A summary of the causes of soil erosion.

(b) Soil erosion in a field in North Norfolk, photographed in February 1987. The erosion was caused by runoff from a field up-slope owned by a different farmer. He had harvested his potatoes in very wet weather, and then drilled winter cereals. The soil was very badly compacted, and rain water collected on the surface of the field, ponding up behind a bank at the field boundary. It then poured over and caused this gully erosion in a neighbouring farmer's field.

How to prevent soil erosion

a) *Improve the vegetation cover on the soil.*

- By deliberate planting, eg. of trees.
- By banning the use of fire.
- By re-seeding pastures.
- By improving the quality of livestock through breeding, supplementary feeds and fodder crops so that fewer animals are kept.
- By using minimum tillage systems, where seeds are sown directly into the earth, without ploughing or harrowing.
- By growing strips of different crops each with different sowing and harvest times so that whole areas are not bare at the same time.
- By growing strips of grass on fields and slopes in between the crops.
- By growing cover crops – one tall crop provides shade and cover for a crop with little ground cover beneath it.

b) *Improve the organic matter of the soil.*

- A lot of the items listed above will do this, as the plant remains decay.
- Plough in crop residues.
- Use more animal manure.

c) *Prevent rapid water run-off down slopes.*

● Build terraces.
● Plough along the contours.
● Build dams of earth or stone across the hillside to trap water.

d) *Prevent wind erosion.*

● Plant rows of trees as wind breaks.
● Replace hedges.
● Plant strips of crops of different height and different harvesting time.

e) *Restrictive measures.*

● Ban felling of trees in certain areas.
● Ban cultivation on steep slopes.
● Restrict the number of cattle grazed in a certain area.

Exercise

1 As a Government Official, where would you start on this list? Write a brief report saying:
  a) what you would do to prevent soil erosion.
  b) how you would get people to adopt these measures. (Would you encourage them, persuade them or force them?)

2 As a poor subsistence farmer, with four children, a few hectares of land and five cattle, which of these things would you be willing to try? What help would you need?

Major ecosystems under threat

We have seen how the world's soils are under threat, but soil is just one part of an ecosystem. There are some major ecosystems in the world which are also threatened in one way or another. The links between parts of the ecosystem were described on page 125. By altering one part of an ecosystem, another part is changed. Some ecosystems are very fragile and are easily destroyed.

The tropical rain forest ecosystem

Exercise

1 Three individual countries contain over half the world's tropical forest (see Figure 5.14(b)). On a world map, shade in the areas of tropical rain forest shown in this figure. Use an atlas to name these three individual countries on your map. Then label South America, Africa, South East Asia and Oceania.

2 Use other maps and diagrams in your atlas to describe:
  a) the position of the tropical rain forests (mention their *latitude*);
  b) the temperature and rainfall conditions in these areas.
  Refer back to pages 119–120 to remind yourself about the climate of these areas. In particular, look up the air pressure conditions, the rainfall totals and the temperatures. Why is the rainfall so heavy in equatorial areas? Pick out the main reason for the heavy rainfall from the three causes of rainfall described on pages 103–104. Page 97 should help you to explain why temperatures are always high.

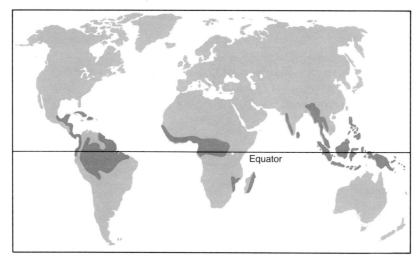

Figure 5.14(a) The location of the world's tropical rain forest.

areas where natural conditions suit the growth of tropical rain forest.
Many of these areas have been cleared and are now used to grow other plants

(b) The importance of the different areas.

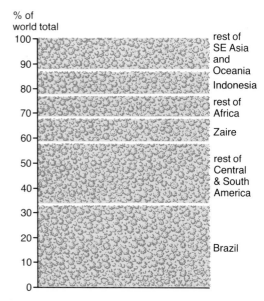

3 Look back to page 127 and find out where most of the nutrients of this ecosystem are stored. Can you suggest why this is called a *fragile ecosystem*?

4 Why and how is the rain forest under threat? Read the extract from an article by Norman Myers (Figure 5.15) published in *The Guardian* on 8 January 1988. Fill in the blanks in the following summary, working out your answers from the article.

Tropical forest is being destroyed and degraded. By the year 2000 a total of .... square miles will be affected in this way. This represents ....% of the total of 3 300 000 square miles of forest today. This is equivalent to removing nearly all of the rain forest in ...., the country which had 33% of the world's total in 1988. The two groups of people named as being responsible for destroying the forests are ..... and ....

5 There are probably about $2\frac{1}{2}$–5 million plant and animal species in the forest. Why does this article suggest it is very important to *keep* all the different plant species found in the tropical rain forests?

Also by the year 2000 we shall have lost at least another 450,000 square miles of tropical forest destroyed outright, and a similar amount of forest degraded, out of remaining forests that today total 3.3 million square miles. Moreover the loss figures suppose that there won't be any acceleration in the present deforestation rate. This is unlikely: the prime agent of deforestation, the slash-and-burn cultivator, is building up his numbers by 3 to 6 per cent per year, due to natural increase of 2.5 per cent or so, the rest being accounted for by landless peasants who migrate into the forests.

As tropical forests go, so do their species. At least half and possibly three-quarters (or even more) of all species occur in tropical forests. Of these, one third or more occur in just 7 per cent of the biome — "hotspot" areas that are both ultra-rich in species and ultra-threatened by the machete and matchbox. In these areas alone we may well lose half a million species by century's end. In other parts of tropical forests, together with wetlands, and other species-rich zones, we shall be fortunate if we do not lose another half million species. Among these "in memoriam" species there could well be several plant species with promising anti-cancer properties, other plants that could serve as sources of new foods, and dozens of animal species that could help with medical research. Some scientists consider that one of the best bets for Aids research lies with the creature from which the virus is thought to have originated, the green monkey of Zaire's forests. Still other scientists believe that anti-Aids drugs could eventually be developed from the Australian chestnut tree.

Figure 5.15 Warnings about the dire consequences of deforestation of the rain forest. *The Guardian* 8.1.88 © Norman Myers

It would be wrong to suggest that it is only local cultivators who are causing the destruction of the rain forest. There are other threats from outside, especially from big business, as Figure 5.16 shows.

In 1987 about 165 000 km² of Amazon forest was burned. About half of this area was virgin forest, in other words it was in its natural state.

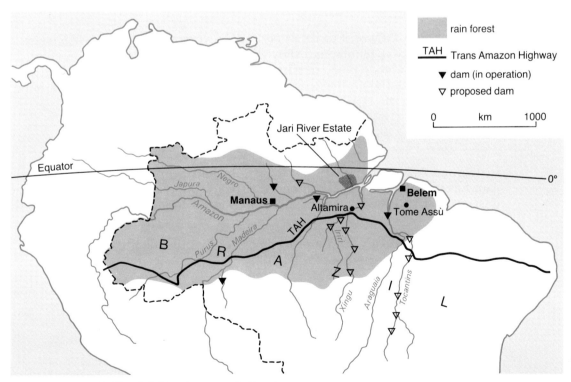

Figure 5.16(a) The shrinking Amazon rain forest.

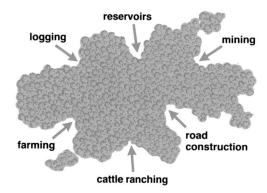

Figure 5.16(b) Forest under threat from attack on all sides.

Deforestation on this scale can have important consequences. For example:

a) Soil erosion may result. A single storm can remove up to 185 tonnes of topsoil from a single hectare which has no tree cover. With the tree cover, much of the rain would reach the ground as a fine spray, while the rest would trickle down the bark and leaves.

b) Soil erosion can lead to silting up of reservoirs. The Ambuklao reservoir in north Luzon, in the Philippines, had its life cut from 60 to 32 years because of rapid silting up.

c) Rainfall may decrease. It is thought that up to half of the rain in the Amazon forest is generated by water evaporated from the forest. As the trees disappear, the amount of evaporated water is reduced.

d) World temperatures may rise. This is partly because of the extra carbon dioxide that will be in the atmosphere, when there are fewer trees to use it. A rise of 2°C by the middle of the next century is not unlikely.

e) The indigenous (local) people would have even fewer areas in which to live. The areas reserved for them to live in are constantly under threat from development.

The rain forest *appears* to be a very fertile, very productive environment. There is a huge variety of plants, and they grow very tall. People have therefore thought that it must be a good place in which to develop farming. The following three case studies illustrate the problems of these developments, and show how farming can be successful in the rain forest.

The Jari River Project, Amazonia

In 1967, an American called D.K. Ludwig bought nearly 12 000 km² of Amazon rain forest for $3 million. He intended to develop forestry for a pulp and paper industry. To do this he had to spend millions more dollars providing all that was necessary:

- A railway system with diesel locomotives to pull wood to the mill.
- Hundreds of kilometres of roads.
- A complete town, called Monte Dourado.
- A pulp mill and a power plant. Both of these were built in Japan and towed across two oceans to Brazil.
- A saw mill.
- A kaolin processing factory to use the kaolin found on the estate.
- A rice growing area together with machinery for harvesting.
- Plantations of Gmelina arborea, a fast growing tree which makes excellent pulp.

The forestry industry was not very successful. In fact the Gmelina trees did so badly that they were replaced with pine and eucalyptus. Even these did not grow as well as expected. Why not? Poor soil fertility is probably the answer. Look at some of the evidence for this in Table 1.

Table 1

	Site One	Site Two
Clearance before planting:	Trees felled, leaves and branches burned. Top soil and charred leaves etc. bulldozed away to make planting easier.	Tree felled, leaves and branches burned Top soil and charred remains left.
Percentage of nutrients removed:	Potassium, 58% Calcium, 80% Magnesium, 67% Phosphorous, 38% Nitrogen, 28%	None – some nutrients reach soil quickly from ash, others slowly from rotting remains.
Harvest:	12 trees averaging 100 kg each, (1,200 kg).	7 trees averaging 280 kg each, (1,960 kg).

Exercise

1 If an area to be planted is completely cleared by bulldozers, what effect will there be on the nutrients in the system? What effect will this have in turn on the yield (crop) of trees?

2 Which nutrients are in shortest supply on the plantations? (Figure 5.17(a).)

3 Biomass is all of the plant matter in an ecosystem. Use Figure 5.17(b) to explain why the biomass is smaller in the two plantations than in the virgin forest.

4 Why would it have been better for D.K. Ludwig to know that most of the nutrients in a rain forest ecosystem are stored in the biomass?

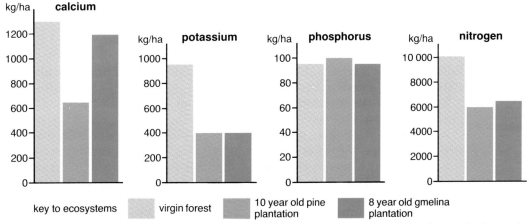

Figure 5.17(a) The amount of nutrients present in three different ecosystems on the Jari estate in Amazonia.

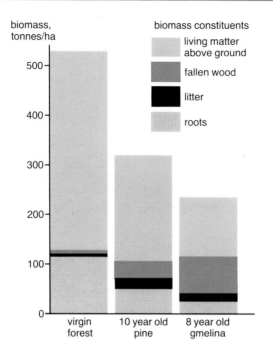

Figure 5.17(b) The amount of biomass in three ecosystems on the Jari estate.

Ludwig sold his estate in 1982. He found that his plantations didn't do as well as he had hoped, and he would have had to spend a huge amount on fertilisers to increase the yield. The trees also suffered fungal attacks. This often happens when only one crop is grown in an area for a long time – a system called *monoculture*.

Agricultural developments along the Trans-Amazon highway

A severe drought hit north east Brazil in 1970. The President of Brazil decided that the Trans-Amazon road should be built to open up the Amazon for farmers hit by the drought – 'to give men without land a land without men'.

The government took over a 100 km wide zone on either side of the road. The part of this nearest to the road was divided into 100 ha plots, each 500 m × 2 km. Each plot cost $700 payable over 20 years, and the government's aim was to have 100 000 families settled there by 1974.

In fact, by 1977 only 7389 families had been established there, and some of them greatly regretted the move, but could not afford to go back to the north east.

Why was this scheme unsuccessful? Several reasons have been given. One is that there were huge transportation problems. Fruit and vegetables could not reach the market quickly enough; instead they rotted. Secondly, the farmers had no means of storing food, and protecting it against pests and predators. Thirdly, and perhaps most importantly, soil fertility was a problem. Figure 5.18 shows the amounts of organic matter, nitrogen and potassium in the soil in five different plots at Altamira.

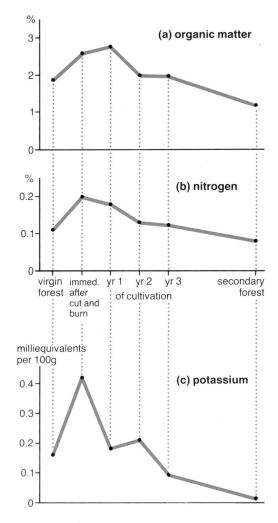

1 What happens to the amounts of nitrogen and potassium in the soil immediately after clearing and burning? Why does this help the farmer?

2 What long term effect does farming have on soil nutrients?

3 What will the farmer have to do after three years of cultivation?

4 Why might farmers not be able to leave each part of their plot long enough for it to recover?

Figure 5.18 Levels of organic matter, nitrogen and potassium in a plot at Altamira near the Trans-Amazon highway.

The shifting cultivators who lived in the forest knew that land must be left long enough to recover before they could use it again. So they knew they had to move their families on to new sites. Settled farmers are fighting a difficult battle, without fertilisers.

Co-operative farming at Tome-Assú, Para, Brazil

This was originally a Japanese colony set up to produce cacao in the early 1900s. Today the farmers produce a variety of products, each farmer growing different things and co-operating with the others. They are also very careful to protect the soil by ensuring that the ground is always covered. Tree crops are grown where only a small part of their biomass is harvested, eg. latex, fruit. This leaves most of the nutrients in the system. High value crops are grown for one year only, as they take a lot of nutrients from the soil. They are followed by less demanding, lower value crops like manioc. As much animal and vegetable organic matter as possible is recycled back into the soil.

This farming settlement in the rain forest is successful. This is partly because of the short distance by road to a market (Belem is only a day away, Sao Paulo four days) and partly because high value crops are grown. The main reason is that the whole ecosystem is being managed very carefully, so that soil fertility does not decline steadily.

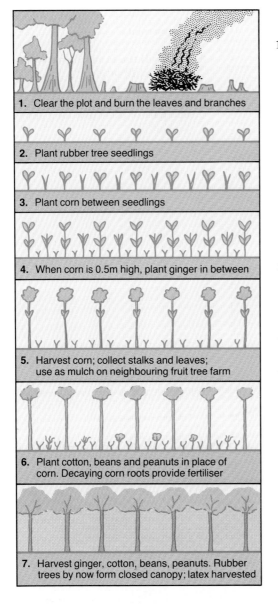

1. Clear the plot and burn the leaves and branches

2. Plant rubber tree seedlings

3. Plant corn between seedlings

4. When corn is 0.5m high, plant ginger in between

5. Harvest corn; collect stalks and leaves; use as mulch on neighbouring fruit tree farm

6. Plant cotton, beans and peanuts in place of corn. Decaying corn roots provide fertiliser

7. Harvest ginger, cotton, beans, peanuts. Rubber trees by now form closed canopy; latex harvested

Exercise

1 Use Figure 5.19(a) and (b) to answer these questions.
   a) Give four different pieces of evidence that nutrients are returned to the soil by these farmers.
   b) Why is it important to keep the ground protected, and how is this done?
   c) Why is nothing grown under a mature rubber plantation?
   d) Give several examples of how the different farms in this colony depend on one another.
   e) Give two reasons why it is better to grow a variety of crops rather than just grow one.

2 Look back at these three examples of rain forest development. Which of them would you consider to be most suitable for the environment? Give reasons for your answer.

3 Which of the three developments is likely to be most popular with the government? Give reasons for your answer.

Figure 5.19(a) A typical crop sequence at Tome-Assú. Note how the ground is always covered, and how one crop is planted before another is harvested.

(b) Links between the different co-operative farms in the Tome-Assú colony.

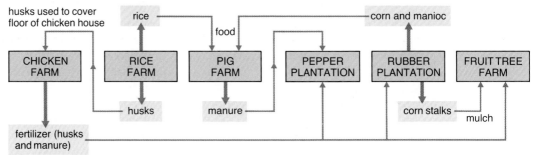

The tundra ecosystem

Compared with the rain forest ecosystem, the *tundra* appears very much less productive. The tundra is the barren land to the far north of North America, Europe and the USSR. Tundra-type ecosystems are also found in high mountains.

The climate experienced in these areas is the polar-type climate described on pages 119–120. Refer back to those pages to remind yourself of the pressure conditions near the poles. You should be able to explain why rainfall totals and temperatures are both low.

Temperatures are cold, particularly in winter. Rainfall is usually less than 250 mm, with slightly more rain in summer than winter. In winter there are long hours of darkness; in summer the days are longer but the sun is never very high in the sky. Temperatures range from −25°C in winter, to 12°C in summer. Beneath the surface layers of soil where small plants and shrubs grow, there is a frozen layer of earth called *permafrost*. This frozen layer prevents drainage of water downwards, so soils may become waterlogged.

The wind, whistling across the tundra plains, is the main factor affecting tundra vegetation. Wind speeds may double between the soil surface and 10–20 cm above the surface. Figure 5.20 shows some of the effects that the wind has on vegetation.

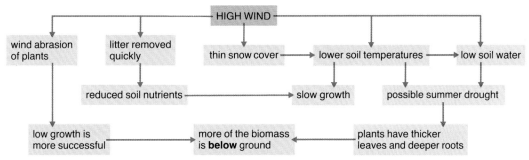

Figure 5.20 Environmental effects on tundra vegetation in northern Alaska.

Exercise

1 Use Figure 5.20 to explain:
   a) Why growth of tundra plants is very slow.
   b) Why low growing plants are found in very windy areas.

2 Draw a new version of Figure 5.20, to show growth conditions likely in a tundra area with low wind speeds.

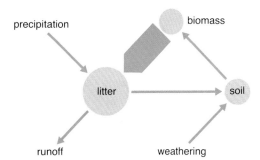

Figure 5.21 Nutrient cycling in the tundra. The diagram shows the amounts of nutrients held in the stores compared with the amounts circulating through the ecosystem.

There are relatively small amounts of nutrients in a tundra ecosystem. This is so for several reasons:

- There is little rainfall to bring in nutrients.
- Rock weathering happens very slowly to release minerals.
- There is little plant material to rot and provide nutrients.

The nutrients that there are in the ecosystem are cycled very slowly, (Figure 5.21), and the plants themselves store a fairly large amount, especially in their roots. Dead plant material rots very slowly to release nutrients into the soil; the *litter layer* is the major store of nutrients. It is also a good insulating layer for the ground.

Threats to the tundra

a) *Reindeer grazing*

This has been happening for many years. The risk is that too many reindeer may be grazed in a particular area. They then eat too much of the vegetation cover and may leave the ground bare. Reindeer need to be moved on from one area to another by the herders. This problem of overgrazing is similar to that experienced in semi-desert areas, which was described on page 137.

b) *Air pollution*

The high pressure conditions in the tundra mean that air tends to sink. Any air pollution, including gases of sulphur dioxide for example, can become trapped at the surface. Sulphur dioxide can do great damage to the tundra vegetation, particularly lichens. The Clean Air Act of 1977 has led to reduction in air pollution in Alaska from pulp mills, power plants and other industries.

The Alaskan Oil Industry

Alaska's oil industry is responsible for about half the employment in Alaska. The Prudhoe Bay field is the largest oil reserve found so far in the USA, and the Alaskan oil fields produce about 16% of the USAs oil production. The high price of oil in the 1970s meant that it was worth drilling for oil, even though the cost was high. Today prices are lower. There had been plans to build an oil refinery in Alaska, but this will not prove worthwhile. This is perhaps a good thing for the Alaskan environment. The oil industry poses several different threats to the environment. There are the problems of building and construction, the effects of vehicles, the pipeline built to carry hot oil south, and the threat of an oil spillage itself.

a) *Building and construction*

The main problem here is the possible melting of the permafrost. If this happens the ground can subside. To prevent this happening, buildings may be placed on gravel pads to insulate them from the ground. Alternatively, piles (massive posts) can be driven into the ground, and frozen into the permafrost. Buildings are then put on platforms supported by these piles. When Inuvik was built in Canada, 20 000 piles cut from the local spruce trees were frozen into the permafrost and used to support the buildings. All major buildings have an air space beneath them of at least 1 m, for further insulation. It was decided to put all piped services inside an insulated box called a *utilidor*, also above ground. Hot water in the heating main helped to ensure that the water main and sewers did not freeze up, (see Figure 5.22).

b) *Vehicles*

Wheeled or tracked vehicles compact the soil and crush vegetation. Destruction of the insulating moss and litter layers can lead to melting of permafrost. Recovery from this sort of damage probably takes hundreds of years in this slowly developing ecosystem. Air cushion vehicles cause less damage, but vegetation may still take two to four years to recover.

c) *The Trans-Alaska pipeline*

This carries hot oil from the north slope to the port of Valdez. It was completed in 1977 and has caused some caribou to alter their migration paths. The pipeline route was chosen very carefully, bearing in mind the risk of earthquakes in Alaska, (see page 20).

d) *Oil spillage*

An oil spillage in the tundra would contaminate the soil, and kill much of the live biomass. The presence of oil in the soil also makes it difficult for plants to extract nutrients from the soil. Wetter sites would suffer less damage as the oil could not soak into the soil so easily.

Exercise

1 Use an atlas to draw a sketch map of Alaska and north west Canada. Mark on it the places named in this section, the Arctic circle, the chief mountain ranges, and the January isotherms.

2 The indigenous people of the Arctic are the Inuit (eskimos). They are called the indigenous population as they have lived there since people first inhabited the area. They are well aware of these threats to the tundra. What do you think their opinion might be? Might there be any benefits to them from the oil industry and associated development?

3 Which other groups of people might be against any further development in the tundra? Give reasons for your answer.

4 Would it be fair to describe the tundra as a fragile ecosystem? Explain your answer.

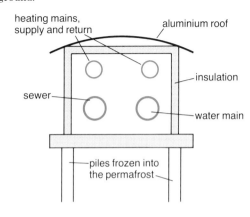

Figure 5.22 A utilidor built in North American tundra towns to carry pipework above the frozen ground.

Antarctica

Antarctica is a continent almost entirely covered by an ice-cap which is four km thick in places. This ice-cap contains about 70% of the world's fresh water. The continent has mountains, some of which have peaks sticking out of the ice-cap (Figure 5.23(a)). It is the only continent never to have been the indigenous home of humans, although it is now home to a population of 1000 or more scientists living in various scientific research stations. It is not a very easy environment in which to live. 98% of the land is covered by the ice-cap, leaving just 2% available

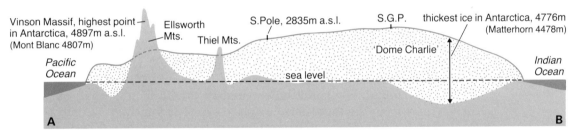

Figure 5.23(a) A cross section across Antarctica. Note the depth of the ice cover.

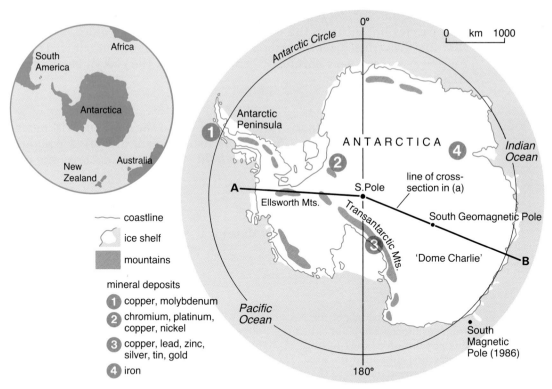

Figure 5.23(b) Antarctica – its political divisions and mineral potential.

for the tundra-type vegetation to grow on. As in the Arctic, this is very fragile. A person's footprint in the Antarctic moss can take years to heal.

In spite of these difficulties, Antarctica (and its resources) is attracting much interest. Why is it attracting such interest?

1 It is a vital part of the earth's climatic system. It is one of the coldest parts of the earth, which helps to drive the whole weather machine. Any melting of the ice-cap could be catastrophic. Not only might it affect climates all over the world, but it would also cause sea levels to rise, and so flood many of the coastal cities of the world.

2 The seas around Antarctica contain huge amount of krill. Krill is a shrimp-like creature up to 7 cm long, and is the major food of many whales, seals, fish, squid and birds. It is at the very centre of the Antarctic food chain (Figure 5.24). It is rich in protein and is eaten in various forms by humans. It can also be made into fish-meal for cattle and poultry. It is already being fished by the USSR, Poland and Japan among others. (Figure 5.25.) The maximum which could be caught in any one year without causing any problems to the natural environment may be 150 million tonnes. At present only a tiny fraction of that amount is caught (about 0.3%). Other fish are also found in large numbers and could be fished economically.

3 Minerals may be found in the rocks of Antarctica. At the moment much of this is guess work. Some minerals have been found but not in quantities that would be worth mining. Oil and gas reserves might also be found as the geological conditions are suitable. The map in Figure 5.23(b) shows the areas which seem to be the most likely sites for minerals to be found in. However, even if large deposits are found, just think how expensive and difficult it will be to mine them. Apart from the fact there is an ice-cap four km thick to drill through, think how far Antarctica is from the markets for minerals. Every single person and thing needed to set up a mine would have to be brought in. Any oil found

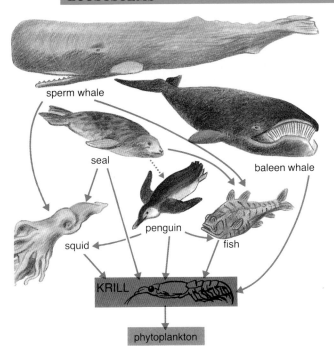

Figure 5.24 The Antarctic food chain.

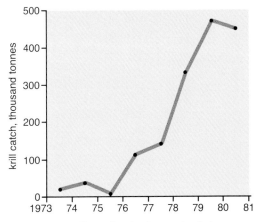

Figure 5.25 Krill catches in Antarctica between 1973 and 1981.

under the ocean would have to be mined in a sea far more treacherous than the North Sea. There is pack ice floating about, the water is deep, and weather conditions are often appalling. Only if every other drop of oil elsewhere in the world had been used, and if we still had not found an alternative fuel, might it be worth the huge cost involved.

4 Antarctica could be a source of fresh water for the rest of the world. Serious suggestions have been made about towing icebergs to parts of the world where there are water shortages. Calculations suggest that even travelling as far as the Middle East enough ice would arrive unmelted to be worth the cost.

5 Antarctica could be the holiday destination for the world-weary traveller who has seen everything else! Already cruise ships visit Antarctica regularly, and tourists visit some of the scientific research stations. Aircraft also bring in visitors.

6 It is a unique area for scientific research. As it is still relatively untouched, it is a good baseline from which to measure amounts of pollution. Ice cores give historical information about air quality. The ozone layer and its changes (see page 123) are being investigated. Geologists are keen to know more about this continent which was at the heart of Gondwanaland (see page 19).

Clearly Antarctica has a number of attractions. Fortunately most people in the world agree that it needs to be protected against developments like these which would threaten it.

In 1959, 12 countries signed the Antarctic Treaty, which set out various rules (called articles) about how Antactica should be used. Since 1959 another six countries have signed the treaty and 14 more have said they are in agreement with it. The most important articles of the treaty are:

1 That the Antarctic should be used for peaceful purposes, (ie. no military bases allowed).
2 That there should be freedom of scientific investigation.
3 That all previous territorial claims to Antarctica should be frozen.
4 That nuclear explosions and the dumping of nuclear waste be prohibited.

Even simply allowing these things to take place is already affecting the Antarctic environment. For example, all the fuel, building materials, machinery and so on needed, has to be brought in by boat, and most of it never leaves. Waste gases from stoves and sewage are both being produced and fed into the Antarctic system. Pieces of level ground with access to the sea are the ones chosen for scientific stations. But there are not many of these, and they are also the areas which plants and breeding penguins inhabit. Any drilling or mining operations would disturb the environment and too much dust or dirt could darken the surface of the continent. This would then affect the amount of radiation reflected back into the sky, which in turn would probably affect the whole world's climate. If krill is over-fished the whales which depend on it will also be threatened. As more people, including tourists, visit Antarctica they bring with them (accidentally) insects, plant seeds and micro-organisms which might have a great effect on the ecosystem.

Because of all these risks, the organisation Greenpeace thinks there should be some different rules for the development of Antarctica. They say:

1 There should be complete protection for all wild life.
2 The protection of the Antarctic wilderness should have first priority.
3 The Antarctic should remain a zone of limited scientific activity.
4 The Antarctic should be a zone of peace.

In effect they would like it to be a world park.

Exercise

1 Use all the resources named here, plus any more you can find, to produce a fact sheet or poster on the preservation of Antarctica, suitable for display on a wall. Try to make the poster eyecatching so that it encourages people to find out why the preservation of Antarctica is important. You could use flow diagrams to illustrate some of the consequences of development.

2 To whom should Antarctica belong? Who should be in charge of developments there? How could this be organised? What are your opinions?

3 Imagine that large amounts of copper are found under Antarctica, and that this metal has become scarce in the rest of the world. Who would be in favour of mining the copper, and why? What problems would they face and how could they overcome them? In your opinion, should the mining be allowed?

Moorland ecosystems in Britain

Closer to home, a third type of threatened ecosystem is the moorland ecosystem in Britain. The section on fire as a factor affecting soil structure (page 131) used the creation of heather moorland as an example. In that instance, humans are deliberately controlling the ecosystem for their own use.

Bracken is a fern which can grow up to 2 m high. It is now found in large areas of upland Britain. The spread of bracken in these areas has not been deliberately encouraged by humans, but it is the result of people's activities. It is now causing a number of problems. It has been estimated that each year about 10 000 ha of upland grazing are lost in Britain because of the spread of bracken.

Exercise

1 Look at Figure 5.26.
   a) Give three reasons why sheep farmers may be unhappy about the spread of bracken.
   b) In what ways might an upland soil improve if bracken grows on it?

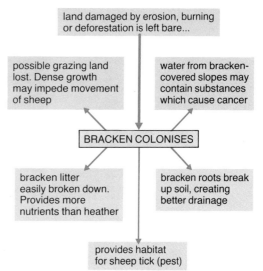

Figure 5.26 Some of the effects of the spread of bracken on Britain's moorland areas.

A second, much larger scale change to upland Britain is conifer planting – *afforestation*. Since 1919, when the Forestry Commission was established, about one million hectares of moorland have been replaced by conifer plantations.

2 Use the map in Figure 5.27 to describe the distribution of Forestry Commission woodland in England, Wales and Scotland. Refer to an atlas map showing relief, and comment on the link between forest distribution and relief.

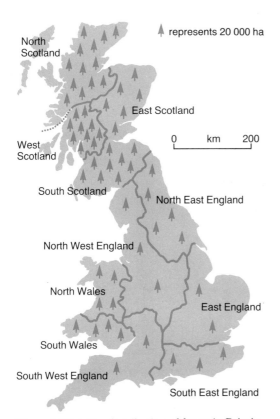

Figure 5.27(a) The distribution of forest in Britain.

Figure 5.27(b) A comparison of the amounts of different types of woodland in England, Wales and Scotland.

The main reason why the Forestry Commission started to plant conifers was to enable Britain to produce more of the wood needed for pulp, paper and building. Their main function is still to produce timber as a commercial enterprise, but they are increasingly taking account of the need to provide a tourist attraction. These two purposes to their work can come into conflict.

Needs of timber production

- Better to have large stands (plots) of one species and one age – easier to fell large areas at once.
- Easier to fell trees if planted in straight rows.
- All land to be used for timber growing.
- Only need tracks for logging vehicles.

Compare these needs of the Forestry Commission with the preferences of over 500 visitors to forests in southern England, who were asked about the sort of forest areas they preferred (Figure 5.28(a)).

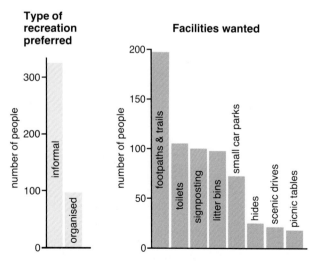

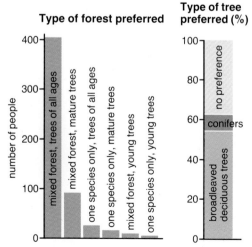

Figure 5.28(a) The types of forest which visitors prefer.

3 You can probably identify at least four conflicts between the needs of the Forestry Commission and the needs of the visitors. What are they?

The Forestry Commission has responded to the views of its visitors, and new plantations are likely to have a greater variety of trees with small groups of one age together. There are also more broad leaved deciduous trees grown, especially on roadsides, at the boundaries of the forest and near picnic areas. Open views are sometimes left at particularly scenic points.

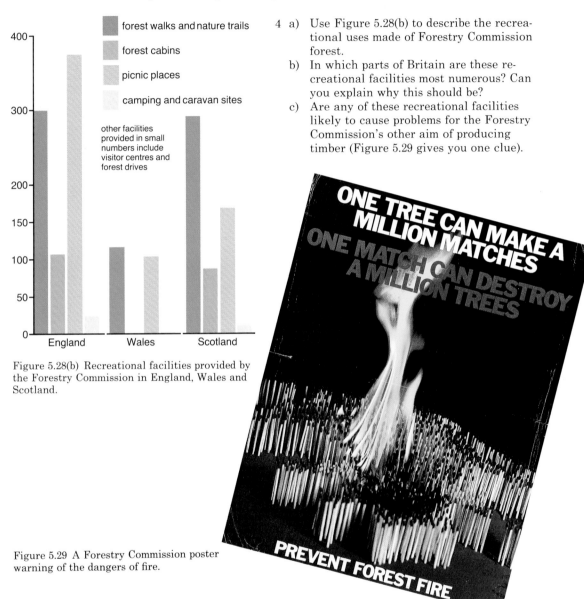

Figure 5.28(b) Recreational facilities provided by the Forestry Commission in England, Wales and Scotland.

4 a) Use Figure 5.28(b) to describe the recreational uses made of Forestry Commission forest.

b) In which parts of Britain are these recreational facilities most numerous? Can you explain why this should be?

c) Are any of these recreational facilities likely to cause problems for the Forestry Commission's other aim of producing timber (Figure 5.29 gives you one clue).

Figure 5.29 A Forestry Commission poster warning of the dangers of fire.

It is also ecologically better for the Forestry Commission to grow more varied types of tree. They run less risk of allowing fungi and pests to destroy a whole forest – the dangers of monoculture have already been described on page 144. Mixed forests are also less likely to be devastated by harsh weather – while some types of tree might be damaged, other types are hardier and will be able to withstand the conditions. A greater variety of types of wood is also easier to sell in different market conditions.

In spite of the changes it has made, the Forestry Commission still receives a lot of criticism for planting too much of Britain's wild, open moorlands with conifers.

A number of planning battles have been fought between conservationist groups like the RSPB, the Wildfowl Trust and the Ramblers Association on the one hand and the Forestry Commission and landowners wishing to plant forests on the other. Recent protests have concerned Criffel in south west Scotland, the Flow country in Sutherland, and the Tweed Valley in the Scottish borders.

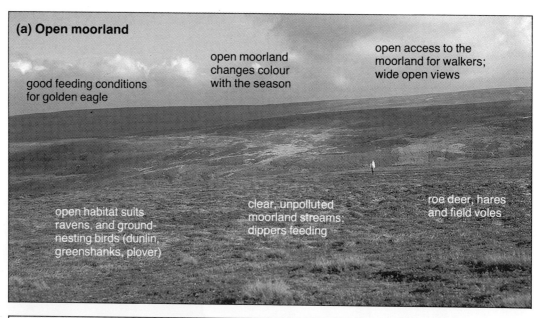

(a) Open moorland

good feeding conditions for golden eagle

open moorland changes colour with the season

open access to the moorland for walkers; wide open views

open habitat suits ravens, and ground-nesting birds (dunlin, greenshanks, plover)

clear, unpolluted moorland streams; dippers feeding

roe deer, hares and field voles

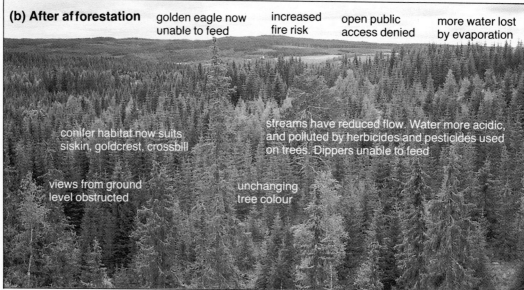

(b) After afforestation

golden eagle now unable to feed

increased fire risk

open public access denied

more water lost by evaporation

conifer habitat now suits siskin, goldcrest, crossbill

streams have reduced flow. Water more acidic, and polluted by herbicides and pesticides used on trees. Dippers unable to feed

views from ground level obstructed

unchanging tree colour

Figure 5.30 The effects of forestry on the landscape.

Exercise

1 Why is an increase in the forested area unpopular? Imagine that you live near the moorland area in Figure 5.30. A local landowner has applied for permission to plant coniferous forest over the area. Write a letter to the landowner explaining why you are unhappy about the proposal. Then try to put yourself on the other side of the argument and write the landowner's reply to you, putting forward the case *for* coniferous planting.

Threats to ecosystems

The effects of acidity on lake and forest ecosystems

Exercise

1 Use Figure 5.31 to find out about and explain:
   a) Three ways in which coniferous trees are damaged by acidity.
   b) The release of and effects of aluminium.

2 Identify a food chain with three levels which is affected by acidity.

3 Explain the ways in which acidity can cause fish to die.

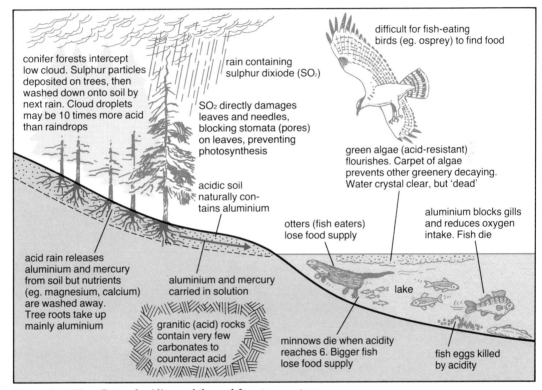

conifer forests intercept low cloud. Sulphur particles deposited on trees, then washed down onto soil by next rain. Cloud droplets may be 10 times more acid than raindrops

rain containing sulphur dixiode (SO_2)

SO_2 directly damages leaves and needles, blocking stomata (pores) on leaves, preventing photosynthesis

difficult for fish-eating birds (eg. osprey) to find food

green algae (acid-resistant) flourishes. Carpet of algae prevents other greenery decaying. Water crystal clear, but 'dead'

acidic soil naturally contains aluminium

aluminium blocks gills and reduces oxygen intake. Fish die

otters (fish eaters) lose food supply

acid rain releases aluminium and mercury from soil but nutrients (eg. magnesium, calcium) are washed away. Tree roots take up mainly aluminium

aluminium and mercury carried in solution

lake

granitic (acid) rocks contain very few carbonates to counteract acid

minnows die when acidity reaches 6. Bigger fish lose food supply

fish eggs killed by acidity

Figure 5.31 The effects of acidity on lake and forest ecosystems.

Acidity – some of the facts

1   In 1900 anglers caught 30 000 kg of salmon in the seven main rivers in southern Norway. Since 1970 *no* salmon have been taken.

2   Salmon cannot survive in water with a pH less than 4.

3   The lowest pH for a single downpour was 2.4 at Pitlochry, Scotland on 10 April 1974.

4   A survey of lakes in Galloway, Scotland in 1979 showed that 26 were so acid that the fish were dying. In Loch Fleet, anglers used to catch 100 trout per annum between 1935 and 1955. Since 1960 no fish have been caught.

5   It is estimated that 18 000 of the 90 000 lakes in Sweden have been badly damaged by acidity.

6   Fishing has been banned in 100 lakes in Sweden because of the high mercury levels in the fish.

7   Trout had been dying in the early 1980s in Lyn Brianne, a reservoir on the River Tywi in Wales. When new trout were introduced into the river they all died within a week.

8   More than a third of West Germany's trees are said to have been damaged by acid rain. The total area affected is about 2 500 000 ha.

9   The trees most badly affected by acidification are fir and spruce.

10   A survey of trees moderately or severely affected by acid rain was made in 1986. It showed 29% of the Netherlands' trees affected, and 16% of the trees in each of Czechoslovakia and Switzerland.

Exercise

1   Mark all the places mentioned in these ten facts on a map of Europe. Add the industrial areas of Midland England, Northern England, the Ruhr in West Germany, and North East France.

2   Illustrate some or all of the ten facts on a poster informing people of the problem.

Table 2 gives some of the effects of acidity on fish and frogs. Figure 5.32 shows the relationship between the pH of streams and the number of pairs of dippers every 10 km. The dipper is a bird about the size of a thrush which lives along fast flowing streams in Britain's uplands. It catches its food by walking along the bottom of the stream to collect caddis and mayflies.

Table 2   The effects of decreasing pH on fish and amphibians

pH	Observations
7.0	
	No effect of pH.
6.5	
	Unlikely to be harmful to fish.
6.0	
	Populations of common frog, natterjack toad and smooth and warty newts encountered less frequently below pH 6. Mortality of natterjack tadpoles noted.
5.5	
	May be harmful to salmonids (salmon, trout, grayling, smelt) if calcium concentration or temperature is low; reproduction of roach may be affected.
5.0	
	Effects on eggs and fry of salmonids and on adults in soft water. May affect common carp. Spawn failure occurring for common frog and common toad.
4.5	
	Effects on salmonids, tench, bream, roach and common carp. Pike may still be able to reproduce. Common toad and palmate newt populations still occur.
4.0	
	Kills salmonids. Tench, perch and pike can survive. Palmate newts recorded down to pH 3.9.
3.5	
	Kills all fish. No reports of amphibian populations breeding at these pH values in Britain.
3.0	

3   Use Table 2 to work out the approximate pH of Loch Fleet since 1960 (fact 4).

4   Which species of fish have greatest tolerance to acidity (ie. they can live in the most acid conditions)?

5 Acidity does not necessarily only wipe out populations through killing the fish or frog itself. How else can it prevent the population continuing?

6 What appears to be the relationship (link) between pH and the dipper population? Why is the dipper unable to find food in an acidic stream?

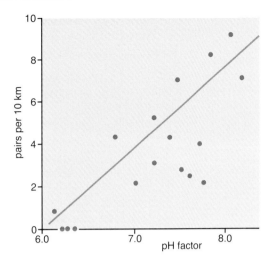

Figure 5.32 The link between the pH of streams and the number of pairs of dippers found along them.

The Forestry Commission is investigating the health of Britain's trees. The colour of needles and leaves is assessed, and measures are made of the size and height of trees, and the amount of loss of foliage. Figure 5.33 shows the results of a survey made in 1986 in Britain and other European countries. The percentage of needle loss from Norway spruce trees is shown. The pecentage losses have been classified as follows:

% needle/leaf loss	Tree health
0–10	Healthy
11–25	Slight damage
26–60	Medium – serious damage
61–99	Dying
100	Dead

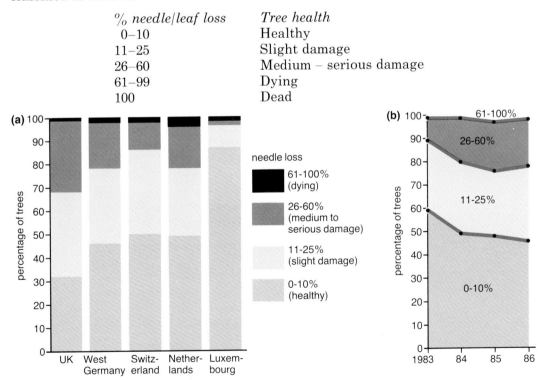

Figure 5.33(a) Needle loss from Norway Spruce trees in five European countries.

(b) Needle loss from Norway Spruce trees in West Germany between 1983 and 1986.

7 What can you tell from Figure 5.33 about the health of Norway spruce trees in these five countries? (Eg. where are they healthiest; least healthy; what percentage is healthy; how much severe damage is there?)

8 What does Figure 5.33 tell you about the *change* in tree health in West Germany between 1983 and 1986?

The Forestry Commission has also tried to explain the increasing damage to trees. They find that there are factors other than acid rain. The other factors include:

a) Extreme climatic conditions, including severe frost or drought. Recent European droughts include those of 1983 and 1984, and the winter of 1986 was very severe.

b) Ozone (O_3). This is *not* the ozone layer described on page 123. There is ozone in the surface air, some of which comes from cars and power stations. Too much ozone is known to cause damage to trees, and might also make the trees weaker so that other factors like acidity in rainwater or air can do them more harm.

c) Soil acidity. Where soils are naturally acidic, for example in highland western Britain, the amount of acidity in the ecosystem is greater. Soils containing a lot of calcium (eg. chalk) can neutralise the acidity as it enters the soil.

d) Fungi and insects. These have been shown to be important in causing damage to pine trees in Britain, although not to spruces.

The most popular argument about tree damage at the moment is that it is caused by *multiple stress*. In other words, there is not one single factor to blame, but a group of factors. As one factor affects the tree, it makes the effect of other factors even greater. Even if acid rain is not the *only* cause of damage to trees, it is still likely to be one of the causes.

Can anything be done to prevent acid damage?
Basically you can either prevent or cure acid damage.

a) Prevention – this would mean reducing emissions of sulphur dioxide and nitrogen oxide using filters of limestone in power stations. It also includes fitting catalytic converters to car exhausts to remove hydro-carbons and nitrogen oxides. These things are being done, but even if all air pollution were stopped tomorrow the effects already noticed would remain for many more years.

b) Cure – by adding limestone to soil and water in huge quantities some of the acidity can be neutralised. However, this limestone can have other effects on plant and animal life. The CEGB (Central Electricity Generating Board) is undertaking a research project at Loch Fleet in Galloway, to bring back trout to the lake. Scientists are using liming and drainage techniques in the catchment area of the lake to reduce its acidity. The lessons they learn there about managing the lake may be used later in other lakes.

Both prevention and cure are necessary – but both cost money!

Exercise

1 Read through the section on air pollution (page 111) again, and this section on acidity in lakes and forests. Imagine a televised debate between two people. One of them is a Biology lecturer who lives in south west Scotland and is keen on fishing. The other is a Director of a company in Sheffield which burns coal to produce power on their site, and which has no way at present of controlling sulphur dioxide emissions from the factory.

Either, work in pairs, each taking one role, and have a discussion about the problem of acidity. Try to explain to the other person what your point of view is. Spend some time preparing your thoughts individually before you begin the discussion.

Or, working alone, write a dialogue between these two people, outlining their views on what, if anything, should be done about acidity.

Desertification

Desertification means that an area of land is made 'like a desert'. It is one of the major crises threatening the world, particularly the semi-arid parts of the world.

Various estimates have been made of the amount of land suffering desertification. Figure 5.34 shows one estimate divided up according to the areas affected in 1977, when a major survey was made by the United Nations.

Since 1977 desertification has spread to an extra 6 000 000 ha every year, making the total area threatened now closer to 310 000 000 ha. Estimates do vary, depending on whether desertification classed as slight, moderate or severe is counted.

There are basically four reasons why land can deteriorate so badly that it loses its vegetation, its nutrients, its water and eventually its soil. Some of these reasons have been described elsewhere in this book (look back to pages 129–131). Figure 5.35 very briefly summarises the chain of events. It would be easy to write 'rapid population growth' across the top of the diagram as the main cause or controlling factor. Population growth is often blamed as the main cause, but this is not necessarily the case. Also, if population growth were the main cause, why is desertification such a problem in North America, which has one of the world's lowest rates of growth?

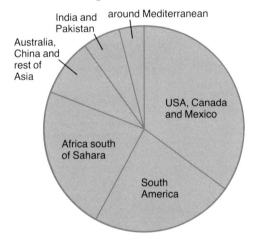

Figure 5.34 Areas of the world threatened by desertification.

Figure 5.35 Causes of desertification.

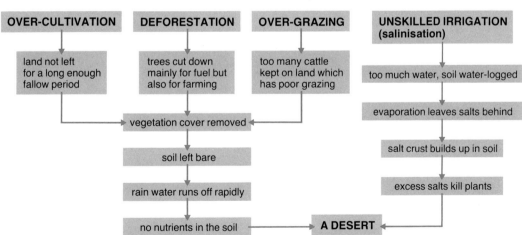

The peasant farmers of the less developed countries are often blamed as the main cause of deforestation. Yet did you know that a North American consumes as much wood in the form of paper each year as the average person in a LDC (Less Developed Country) burns for fuel? Of course, the wood cut for the North American to use may be cut from a less fragile ecosystem.

Over grazing may result, as it did in Ethiopia, from a desire to use the best land, ie. flood plain, to produce cash crops. Forcing the herders on to more marginal land has led to desertification.

Drought is also frequently blamed for desertification. Drought may well be the *trigger* which encourages desertification, but until we put so much extra pressure on the land droughts could be survived.

In North America, the dust bowl conditions which returned in 1988 were partly the result of a drought, but they also occurred because the land was being farmed without enough care being taken to store soil moisture.

So it is too easy to blame these processes of desertification on one thing. There are many causes contributing to desertification. It may even result from changes people make to try to *improve* food production. Recent events in Uzbekistan in the USSR illustrate this.

The Aral Sea, Uzbekistan

The Aral Sea is an inland sea which used to be about the same size as Scotland north of a line joining Glasgow and Edinburgh. The Aral Sea is shrinking fast. It has lost 60% of its water in 30 years. By 2010 it will be only 8% of its size in 1960. Sea level has fallen by 12 m. A former port, Muinak, is now 50 km from the edge of the water. Rusting fishing boats lie forlornly on the sand dunes surrounding the lake.

Figure 5.36 The shrinking Aral Sea, USSR, showing the original system and the alterations to it.

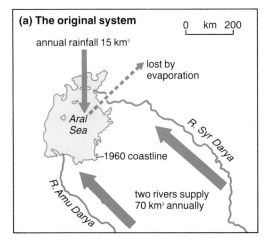

(a) The original system

0   km   200

annual rainfall 15 km³

lost by evaporation

Aral Sea

R. Syr Darya

1960 coastline

R. Amu Darya

two rivers supply 70 km³ annually

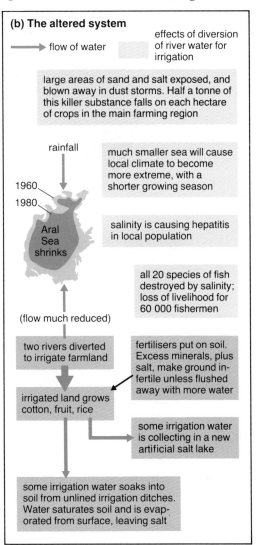

(b) The altered system

→ flow of water

effects of diversion of river water for irrigation

large areas of sand and salt exposed, and blown away in dust storms. Half a tonne of this killer substance falls on each hectare of crops in the main farming region

rainfall

1960
1980

Aral Sea shrinks

much smaller sea will cause local climate to become more extreme, with a shorter growing season

salinity is causing hepatitis in local population

all 20 species of fish destroyed by salinity; loss of livelihood for 60 000 fishermen

(flow much reduced)

two rivers diverted to irrigate farmland

fertilisers put on soil. Excess minerals, plus salt, make ground infertile unless flushed away with more water

irrigated land grows cotton, fruit, rice

some irrigation water is collecting in a new artificial salt lake

some irrigation water soaks into soil from unlined irrigation ditches. Water saturates soil and is evaporated from surface, leaving salt

Figure 5.37 Fishing boats abandoned in the desert which used to be the bed of the Aral Sea.

Exercise

1 The Aral always was a salty sea. Use Figure 5.36 to explain why.

2 What was the main cause of the shrinkage of the Aral Sea?

3 What 'mistakes' were made when setting up this irrigation scheme?

4 The original irrigation scheme had some un-foreseen consequences. What were they?

Cape Verde

Most Governments now realise the importance of preventing desertification, and of regaining the land they have already lost. The newspaper extract in Figure 5.38 gives details of one small success story, admittedly on a tiny island off the west coast of Africa, Cape Verde, but none the less important.

WHEN rains begin falling in the tiny African country of Cape Verde, the entire population roll up their sleeves and set to work in the mud. They have 10 days to plant three million trees.

Although it is virtually an off-shore extension of the Sahara desert, Cape Verde has managed to plant 17 million trees since independence in 1975, even with a 20-year drought which ended with good rains in 1987. Despite the droughts, there has been no recurrence of the last severe famine in the 1940s which left almost 20,000 people dead.

Forestry experts say trees are crucial to drought-stricken areas because they stop erosion of the soil, hold water, provide firewood and eventually modify the micro-climate.

Cape Verde, a former Portuguese colony which was until recently one of the world's poorest countries, gets an average of 300 mm of rain per year, all of it within about 10 days in August. Weather during the rest of the year is hot, dry, and windy.

Driving around Sao Vicente, one of the most barren of Cape Verde's 10 islands, dusty brown hills are suddenly broken by a burst of green coconut and mango trees in an enclosed area fed by a well and protected by walls against the wind. Although the islands vary greatly and landscapes range from lush valleys to flat, dry salt pits, water is lacking everywhere.

"The basic problem here is water. But on the whole, it's much better than other places in Africa. You don't have the desert slowly taking over," said Mr Willy Salters of the US Agency for International Development.

Cape Verdians are also building dams, dykes, wells, and watersheds — walls staggered along valleys to help stop rain from rushing down the mountains straight into the sea. Experiments are under way in solar and wind energy and a USAID project is even trying to collect water from fog.

Despite their successes, Cape Verdian officials admit they have far to go before they have the land covered in vegetation. Only about one tenth of the country's surface is planted.

"There is a tremendous respect for trees here, even at the lowest level of society," Mr Meloni said. "You will never see a person cutting down a tree. You will see them trimming carefully. To the Cape Verdians, trees are like beautiful flowers."

Figure 5.38 The benefits of afforestation in Cape Verde.

Exercise

1 In what ways does it appear that the people of the country are backing the Government's attempts to prevent desertification?

2 What other methods are being used to make maximum use of the scarce rainfall resources?

3 What improvements have already been achieved in Cape Verde?

4 As desertification is such a severe problem, we need to consider how to prevent it. Look at Figures 5.35 and 5.36 and the relevant sections of this book dealing with over-cultivation, deforestation and over-grazing.

Look at the causes of each of these problems, and consider how the causes could be reversed. In other words, think about examples of good practice which would not lead to desertification. Draw up a ten point plan suitable to present to a government explaining how they could prevent further damage. Include suggestions on how they could improve the quality of the land already damaged.

5 If we do not act now to halt desertification, what might some of the consequences be?

Checklist of Key ideas

Key ideas	Examples
Chapter 1	*Chapter 1*
The environment can be both a resource and a hazard.	People are attracted to live on floodplains because of the fertility of the soil, but the possibility of the river flooding is a hazard.
Parts of the environment function as systems which are interlinked.	Removal of shingle off shore contributed to coastal erosion at Hallsands.
A system has inputs, storage zones and outputs.	The water cycle is a well known system.
Alterations to a system can have unforeseen effects.	The Bakolori Dam in Nigeria has made farming more hazardous for some farmers.
Disasters can be classified into different types, and have a bigger impact in some countries than others.	Asia suffers much greater loss of life through disasters than North America.
Chapter 2	*Chapter 2*
The rocks of the earth's crust all form part of a large rock cycle and are interlinked.	A sand grain weathered from granite could form part of a sedimentary rock, sandstone, which might then be metamorphosed to make quartzite.
The theory of plate tectonics helps to explain the structure of the earth.	Mountains, volcanoes and earthquakes are found at certain types of plate boundary.
The extent of disasters caused by volcanoes varies from one place to another.	Mount St. Helens caused much less loss of life when it erupted than did Nevado del Ruiz.
Volcanoes are like other physical systems in that they provide resources as well as hazards.	Minerals, tourist attractions, fertile soil and geothermal power are all potential benefits of volcanic regions.
Prediction of a volcanic eruption or an earthquake can help to reduce loss of life.	Evacuation from the Mount St. Helens area reduced loss of life when it erupted.
Chapter 3	*Chapter 3*
The landscape can be divided into smaller systems, but these are still interlinked.	The processes operating on a slope can have an effect on a river valley, as they did above the Vaiont Dam.
Human intervention in a physical system can contribute to a disaster.	The development of ski resorts in the Valtellina valley contributed to the mud avalanching experienced in 1987.

Key ideas	Examples
Only by understanding the workings of a physical system, can people gauge the likely effect of any changes they make to the system.	An understanding of the water cycle helps us to work out the effect on a river's hydrograph of building a town.
Some processes of erosion and deposition are common to several physical systems, and they help to produce a set of distinctive features.	The valley shapes typical of river erosion are different from those typical of glacier erosion.
The use of the natural environment for tourism is increasing, but puts an additional pressure on the various systems and can cause problems.	Rock climbing on sea cliffs, building ski resorts in upland Britain and the use of the Norfolk Broads for holiday boats, can all contribute to environmental problems.
Human use of the environment can encourage us to try to maintain landscape features in their present form, and stop them developing as they normally would.	We try to control the position of the Mississippi river, and to maintain Spurn Head in its present location. Both features have a history of forming, being destroyed and reforming. We aim to prevent this natural cyclic change.
Chapter 4	*Chapter 4*
In the same way that landscape systems are linked, so are all the processes which control weather and climate.	A change in the output of heat from the sun can affect temperature and rainfall conditions world wide.
Humans can affect both temperatures and rainfall accidentally or by deliberate actions.	The building of cities may increase rainfall, and cloud seeding is a method of deliberately achieving the same effect.
The effect of changes to the atmosphere may be felt a long way from the site of the input.	Acid rain damage is particularly great in Norway and Sweden, probably as a result of air pollution in Britain.
Changes humans make to the atmosphere probably have very long term consequences, which we can only guess at.	The importance of the ozone layer is now recognised, and attempts are being made to stop its destruction. However the effects of damage already done may be with us into the next century.
Economic activities come to depend on a particular set of average rainfall and temperature conditions, and can be disrupted when these take an extreme value.	The 1976 drought in Britain, or the El Nino events in Peru are both examples of events that disrupted economic life.
Chapter 5	*Chapter 5*
The biosphere can be divided up into ecosystems which have similar structures, but whose components vary in importance.	Ecosystems consist of living parts including producers, consumers and decomposers and non-living parts including soil, air and water.

Key ideas	Examples
The cycling of nutrients in the ecosystem is vital in keeping it healthy. When nutrients are removed, the ecosystem begins to deteriorate.	The plantations on the Jari River estate were unsuccessful in the long run.
Soil erosion is a direct consequence of the breakdown of soil stucture, which can happen for a number of different reasons.	Soil erosion on English farms and in the Khumbu valley in Nepal provide just two examples from many.
A fragile ecosystem is one which can deteriorate quickly when it is interrupted. This might be because most of the nutrients are moving through the ecosystem rather than being held in stores within it, or because the rate of nutrient cycling is very low.	Two examples of fragile ecosystems are the rain forest and the tundra.
Ecosystems, like landscape and climate systems, also provide resources for human use, particularly for food production.	Co-operative farming in Brazil or cattle grazing in Ethiopia for example.
Ecosystems are under threat from various human activities, including farming, mining and recreational uses.	The character of moorland Britain is changing as a result of several economic pressures.

Glossary

abrasion – the wearing away of rock by water, wind or ice which contains particles of sand.

afforestation – the deliberate planting of trees in an area where there were none before.

alluvium – the fine sand and silt which a river has carried and eventually deposited. An alluvial soil is a very fertile one.

air mass – a mass of air which covers a huge area. The whole mass has similar temperature and moisture conditions throughout its area. A polar air mass, for example, is one which has come from the poles and will contain cold, dry air.

anticyclone – a weather system which has high pressure at its centre

arête – a sharp, knife-edged ridge found in glaciated areas, often formed between two corries.

attrition – the process of breaking down rock particles into smaller pieces as they hit against one another when being carried by water, wind or ice.

backwash – the flow of sea water back down a beach after a wave has broken.

biomass – the amount of living matter in an ecosystem.

biosphere – the part of the Earth's surface occupied by living things

carnivore – an animal which eats the flesh of other animals.

chlorophyll – the green colouring matter of plants.

cold front – the boundary between a cold air mass and a warm air mass. It is found in the rear of a depression where cold air is being pushed into warm air, so that the warm air is lifted off the ground.

condensation – the process which happens when air containing water vapour (an invisible gas) cools. As the air cools, the water vapour turns back into droplets of water, which can be seen.

deforestation – the removal of trees from a large area.

depression – a weather system with low pressure at its centre. Also known as a cyclonic system.

desertification – the process of making land desert-like, for example by removing the vegetation, causing soil erosion or removing soil moisture.

distributary – one of the channels which a river divides into as it flows across a delta into the sea.

drainage basin – the area of land surrounding a river, and its tributaries, which drains into that river. The edge of the drainage basin is marked by its watershed.

evaporation – the process which happens when water is heated enough to turn it into a gas, known as water vapour.

evapotranspiration – the total loss of water from the soil. Part of the loss comes from evaporation from water and the soil, and part comes from the transpiration of plants.

exfoliation – a weathering process in which layers of a rock peel off. It is partly caused by alternate expansion and contraction of the surface of the rock due to changes in temperature in hot desert areas.

fault – a plane of weakness in a rock mass or in the earth. It may be a few centimetres or several hundred kilometres long. The ground on either side of the fault can move independently.

fetch – the distance over which a sea wave has travelled before it reaches the shore.

fracture plane – another term for a fault in part of the earth's crust.

frost-shattering – a weathering process caused by the freezing of water in crevices in a rock face. As the water freezes it expands and puts pressure on the surrounding rock, causing some pieces to be shattered. Also known as freeze-thaw weathering.

geothermal power – electricity produced by hot water or steam which occurs naturally in the earth's crust.

herbivore – an animal which eats only plant and vegetable materials.

histogram – a graph used to show the frequency of particular events.

humus – decomposed plant and animal matter in the soil. Humus is organic matter ie. it was once living.

hydraulic action – the erosion of land by the force of water itself.

hydro-electric power – electricity produced by the force of water turning a turbine.

hydrograph – a graph drawn to show the flow of water in a river. The hydrograph may be for a whole year, or for a few hours marking a single rain storm.

impermeable – a rock which does not allow water to soak into it. Granite is an example.

infiltration – the process in which rain water soaks into the soil.

interception – the catching of rain water by the leaves, branches and stems of plants and trees.

irrigation – the artificial addition of extra water to the soil by means of pipes, buckets, sprinklers, canals etc.

latent heat – the heat used to evaporate water. This heat is stored in the vapour. When the vapour condenses back to a liquid, the latent heat is released.

leaching – the process in which soluble minerals are washed out of the soil by rain water.

litter layer – the layer of dead and decaying plant and animal matter lying on the surface of the soil. When this material is mixed into the soil it forms humus.

magma – molten rock inside the earth's crust. When it emerges at the surface it is called lava.

magnitude – the magnitude of an earthquake is a measure of its energy and power. It is worked out from the size of the waves recorded on the seismograph. It can be measured on the Richter scale.

moraine – the general name for rock debris of all sizes deposited by ice.

organic matter – that part of the soil which used to be, or still is, living, including both plants and animals.

permafrost – a layer of permanently frozen ground in Arctic areas. The surface soil layers may melt each summer, but below a certain depth the ground will remain frozen. At the bottom of the permafrost layer, the heat from inside the earth will keep the rocks unfrozen.

permeable – a rock which will allow water to pass through it, for example sandstone.

photosynthesis – the conversion by plants of carbon dioxide and water from the air into carbohydrates. The process only happens in the presence of light. Plants which can photosynthesize are producing their own food, hence they are called producers.

polar front – the boundary between polar air and tropical air; it is located at about 60° North and South.

porous – a rock which contains minute holes, or pores, which let water pass through it. Chalk is an example.

precipitation – the name given to all ways in which water from the atmosphere can fall to earth, including rain, snow, hail, and fog.

pressure gradient – the rate at which air pressure changes from one place to another. It is shown by the spacing of isobars. If the isobars are close together, the pressure gradient is steep and the wind speed will be high.

radiation – the process by which a body emits heat. The sun emits solar radiation all the time. The earth's surface can also emit radiation when it has been warmed by the sun.

Richter scale – a scale used to measure the magnitude of earthquakes. It is a logarithmic scale, so an increase of one on the scale means a tenfold increase in the magnitude of the earthquake.

runoff – the process in which rain water travels over the ground surface, towards the sea.

salinisation – the process which makes surface layers of the soil very salty. It happens when there is a lot of evaporation from waterlogged soil. As the pure water evaporates, the mineral salts are left behind. Careless irrigation can lead to salinisation.

seismograph – an instrument used to measure earth movements, in particular earthquake shocks.

smog – a deadly combination of smoke and fog found in some industrial cities. In Britain it is less common than it was, due to various Clean Air Acts.

solifluction – the flow of soil down a slope, particularly in the tundra. The wet surface layers of soil flow down over the frozen ground beneath.

swash – the flow of sea water up the beach as a wave breaks.

temperature range – the difference in degrees between the highest and lowest temperature.

throughflow – the water which flows through the soil downhill towards a river.

tidal range – the difference in height between low tide and high tide level.

transpiration – the process by which plants take water from the soil, pass it up through their stems to the leaves, from where it is evaporated.

tributary – a stream or river which flows into a larger one.

tsunami – a very large sea wave caused by an under-sea earthquake. They are experienced in Japan and other areas bordering the Pacific Ocean.

viscous lava – lava which is very thick and does not flow smoothly. Lavas which are granitic are usually viscous. Basaltic lavas are not viscous.

warm front – the boundary between a warm air mass and a cold one. It is found at the front of a depression, where warm air is being pushed towards and over cold air.

watershed – the boundary line drawn on a map around one drainage basin. Any precipitation landing inside the watershed of a particular river's drainage basin would find its way eventually into that river.

water table – the upper level of water stored underground in rocks.

Index

Place index